AMERICAN CIVIL RELIGION: AN ASSESSMENT

D0094173

by
GAIL GEHRIG

Lewis University
Romeoville, Illinois

SOCIETY FOR THE SCIENTIFIC STUDY OF RELIGION
MONOGRAPH SERIES
NUMBER 3

Library of Congress Catalogue Card Number: 81-82801
International Standard Book Number: 0-932566-02-2

Editor's Introduction

Religious idea systems possess an apparently unique capacity to provide cultural unity in the face of social diversity. This, of course, was a consistent theme in the writings of the 19th century social theorists. Whether religion continues to play this kind of social role, and in what forms it does so, has become a focal point of often-heated debate among contemporary sociologists, historians, and theologians. At the vortex of these debates has been the concept of "civil religion."

By comparing the various empirical and theoretical writings on civil religion, this monograph provides a long-needed conceptual map for examining these issues. The goal here is not so much to end so-called civil religion debate, but to bring order and clarification to this diverse literature. The SSSR Monograph Series is indeed pleased to have this valuable contribution as Volume 3 in our Series.

William M. Newman
Editor

Norwich, CT
July 6, 1981

TABLE OF CONTENTS

LIST OF FIGURES

CONTENTS OF APPENDIX

PREFACE

The idea for a book on American civil religion originated in my concern about the present state and future direction of American society. As a sociologist I want to understand the structures and processes of American society. As an individual citizen I have been impressed by American myths, symbols, and ideals. Both perspectives coalesce in the study of American civil religion. My assessment of the American civil religion literature has exposed me to the ideas of scholars whom I have not met, yet with whom I nevertheless feel well acquainted. I believe I know something of significance about each scholar because I have been exposed to his vision concerning the mythic structure of the nation. It seems appropriate that i also share some background concerning my own perspective on American civil religion.

I am a member of the post-World War II baby boom generation of young adults who grew up in the promising era of national well-being of the 1950s and early 1960s. Like many members of my generation, I experienced the blessings my country offered, and I perceived America to be truly "one nation, under God, indivisible, with liberty and justice for all." I was not the only member of my generation to feel betrayed when America seemed to fail to live up to these ideals. The Berkeley free speech movement of the early 1960s raised questions about the extent to which Americans valued personal freedom. America's involvement in the Vietnamese war challenged my conceptions of liberty and justice. By the late 1960s American society no longer had the appearance of indivisibility. At that time I did not realize that I was experiencing a common American historical occurance, later to be symbolized by Robert Bellah as the broken American covenant.

Throughout the deep national polarization characteristic of the Vietnamese war era I was curious to determine if there was a basic value system common to Americans. Was there an American collective conscience underlying the ideological conflict? Americans seemed to agree upon a general set of national ideals, but were divided on the interpretation of those ideals. American involvement in Vietnam could be interpreted as a noble effort to preserve the values of freedom from oppression, or, conversely, as an oppressive attempt to limit Vietnamese national self-determination. In either interpretation, "freedom and justice for all" was the symbolic concern.

The American paradox of value unity underlying value diversity was personally compelling because I was an active participant in the national value conflict. My father, who supported American involvement in Vietnam, and I, who protested that involvement, shared a thin thread of common values about the ultimate purpose of our nation. My father and I both believed that America has a moral duty to embody the ideals of freedom and justice in the world. My intellectual interest in

American civil religion began with my private effort to bridge the divided American generations. I have come to realize that despite our different ideologies, my father's and my generations are spiritual natives of the same homeland.

When I first began researching the American civil religion literature I found an ocean of unsystematized ideas. Numerous scholars, representing diverse fields, have expressed interest in civil religion, but share no single common definition of the concept. Some scholars doubt that American civil religion exists as an objective social fact. Others are convinced of the viabilty of American civil religion as a sociological concept, but disagree on appropriate measurement techniques. Before I could study American civil religion further it would be necessary to systematize the confusing wealth of ideas and opinions.

Landmarks in the American civil religion literature which particularly stimulated me include Robert Bellah's *The Broken Covenant,* followed by Richard Fenn's critique, "Bellah and the New Orthodoxy." Both works address what I consider to be the central sociological question in the study of American civil religion. Is American civil religion religious, or is it merely ideology? This book does not explicitly answer that question, but provides instead many answers and many more questions, presented in a manner designed to provoke further thought and research.

I am also indebted to John A. Coleman for his typology of civil religion and his set of civil religion propositions. Coleman provides a cross-cultural framework for the comparative analysis of civil religious systems which I believe is crucial to the understanding of civil religion in American society.

The study of American civil religion has provided me with a means of integrating a personal quest for self-understanding with a sociological curiosity. Questions about the meaning of my own life are tied to questions about my relationship to my society and to the ultimate meaning of that society's role in history. My work on this book has helped me develop a framework for structuring these questions. I hope the book will be of use to others who share my concerns and will provide a foundation for the generation of further inquiry.

ACKNOWLEDGEMENTS

This book was originally written as a Ph.D. dissertation for the Sociology Department at Loyola University of Chicago. I wish first to thank my thesis director, Professor Robert N. McNamara, and the members of my committee, Rev. Thomas M. Gannon, S. J. and Professor Ross P. Scherer for their assistance and advice on the original manuscript. I am greatly indebted to the editorial staff of the Society for the Scientific Study of Religion Monograph Series, and specifically to the editor, William Newman, whose perceptive suggestions enabled me to develop a dissertation into a book. I wish to thank as well Gail Langer, who assisted me with the index and bibliography. Finally, I want to express appreciation to my husband, Jacob Spitz, and to my parents, for their sustaining love and encouragement.

CHAPTER 1

INTRODUCTION

A. An Overview

Civil religion, a term first used by Rousseau, refers to the religious dimension of the polity. Civil religion in American society has been the subject of an extensive field of literature generated since the inception of the nation by philosophers, historians, theologians, social scientists, poets, and novelists. Stimulated by the work of Robert Bellah, the concept of American civil religion has recently generated interest among American sociologists, leading to a sociological debate on American civil religion. The debate is wide-ranging, beginning with disagreement about the definition of American civil religion and its existence in American society. Even among sociologists who accept the assumption that American civil religion exists, there is still considerable controversy over the historical origin and continued development of American civil religion. There is also fierce debate on such issues as the structural differentiation of American civil religion from other social institutions, and on the functions (if any) performed by American civil religion. The purpose of this book is to examine the social science literature on American civil religion and to organize these materials into a coherent, comprehensive, and logical set of definitions and assumptions open to empirical examination. This book does not attempt to assemble a patchwork quilt comprised of every piece ever written about American civil religion, or to present a strictly chronological history of the literature. Rather, the purpose is to construct a representative theoretical map of the most significant American civil religion studies, and to glean from these studies a set of propositions that would be testable by sociological methods.

B. Defining American Civil Religion

This assessment of the American civil religion literature is organized conceptually around five definitions, or models, of American civil religion, which are compared and evaluated. The literature is selectively reviewed, with representative studies examined as typical of a particular model. Evaluation of the models provides the basis for defining American civil religion in sociological terms, and for developing sociological propositions concerning the structural and functional differentiation of American civil religion. The ideas of major contributors to the American civil religion debate appear and reappear throughout the book. Each contributor's model of American civil religion is briefly sketched in the opening chapters, and elaborated upon in increasing detail as the analysis procedes. Chapter two lays the foundation for defining American civil religion by tracing the intellectual history of the concept. The contributions of philosophers and historians which have had the greatest impact on the sociological study of American civil religion are highlighted. Chapter three builds on this foundation by examining major theoretical and empirical contributions to the sociological literature on American civil religion.

C. Models of American Civil Religion

Richey and Jones suggest a conceptual schema which is helpful for the organization of the American civil religion literature (1979:14-17). They find five different definitions of American civil religion prevalent in the literature: folk religion, transcendent religion of the nation, religious nationalism, democratic faith, and Protestant civic piety. The five definitions can be viewed as models and used collectively as an organizing device to facilitate the comparison of different American civil religion studies. Because the five models are not mutually exclusive, some studies contain elements of more than one model. However, the majority of studies can be usefully classified as representative of a particular model.

1. Folk Religion

Folk religion is a civil religion emerging from the daily life experiences and expressions of the American populace. The major functions of folk religion are legitimation of cultural values, and social integration. Alexis de Tocqueville's two-volume work, *Democracy in America,* contains one of the first intellectual developments of American folk religion. During his contact with the American people in the 1830s, Tocqueville observed that a fusion of democratic and moral principles was expressed in the daily behavior and customs of Americans. A classic sociological analysis of American folk religion is found in W. Lloyd Warner's (1961) examination of the Memorial Day celebrations in an American city. Other descriptions of folk religion include Will Herberg's (1955) analysis of the deification of the American way of life, Martin Marty's (1959) religion-in-general, and Andrew Greeley's (1972) definition of folk religion as the popularized religion of reassurance and conformity.

2. Transcendental Universal Religion of the Nation

The transcendent universal religion of the nation model portrays American civil religion as a set of transcendent ideals by which the society is both integrated and judged. Due to its prophetic capacities, transcendent universal religion is capable of greater challenge to society than folk religion. Religious historian Sidney Mead's (1963;1967) religion of the republic is an example of the transcendent universal model. It consists of a synthesis of democratic and deistic values which challenge both sectarianism and national self-transcendence. In 1967 Robert Bellah introduced a sociological model of transcendent universal American civil religion. Bellah's model proposes that American civil religion exists as an institutionalized collection of sacred beliefs, providing sources of cohesion and prophetic guidance through times of national crisis. He cites examples of the unifying and prophetic manifestations of American civil religion throughout American history. In later writings, he notes that, at times, the symbols of American civil religion have also been misused for national self-reinforcement and self-transcendence (Bellah, 1975;1976b). The folk religion model is thus partially contained within the transcendent universal model, with folk religion representing the distortion of universal ideals into national public theology. Greeley (1972;166) calls the transcendent universal model "elite" civil religion, representing the highest ideals of the nation. The transcendent universal model of American civil religion has stimulated the greatest amount of contemporary inquiry.

3. Religious Nationalism

The third model of American civil religion noted by Richey and Jones (1974:16) is religious nationalism. Religious nationalism represents a worldview in which the nation itself is glorified and adored, becoming self-transcendent. The idolatrous component is highly manifest in the model of religious nationalism, as compared to the latent national self-transcendence of folk religion. There has been little systematic examination of religious nationalism as a distinct model of American civil religion. Religious nationalism has been depicted as the opposite of the transcendent universal model (Bellah, 1975), or as folk religion taken to its most idolatrous extreme (Marty, 1959;1974).

4. Democratic Faith

The democratic faith model of American civil religion is primarily represented in the writings of philosophers and theologians who have attempted to construct a humanistic philosophy based on the American ideals of justice, liberty, and equality. Democratic faith typically refers neither to a transcendent authority nor to a self-transcendent nation, and is thus more a humanistic value system than a transcendent religion. The common faith of John Dewey (1934) is a classic example of democratic faith. Dewey's common faith was based on the conscious and dedicated pursuit of democracy. Dewey's common faith best serves as an example of how the humanistic values of American civil religion could be embodied in the personal value system of an individual citizen.

5. Protestant Civic Piety

Richey and Jones (1974:17-18) note that a particular model of American civil religion, Protestant civic piety, is found in the works of historians such as James Smylie (1963), Winthrop Hudson (1970), Robert Michaelson (1970), and James Maclear (1971). Protestant civic piety emphasizes that the origin of American civil religion can be found in the fusion of the American and Protestant historical traditions. Protestant civic piety typically contains the following elements: (a) the theistic conception of a transcendent authority for the nation; (b) the legitimation of Protestant values as applied to national life; and (c) the integration of Protestant citizens as Americans. Although Protestant civic piety is the least comprehensive of the five models of American civil religion, the model is explored in some detail in chapter two because Protestant civic piety has historical importance for tracing the origins of American civil religion.

Because the transcendent universal model of American civil religion is the most comprehensive of the five models and has received the most theoretical and empirical attention from contemporary sociologists, it will serve as the basic model for the derivation of a sociological definition of American civil religion. John A. Coleman (1970:69) proposes a definition of civil religion derived from the transcendent universal model of Bellah. In chapter three Coleman's definition is applied to the American case, defining American civil religion as the religious symbol system which relates the citizen's role and American society's place in space, time, and history, to the conditions of ultimate existence and meaning. This proposed definition has utility for generating further assumptions about American civil religion which could be tested by sociological methods.

Once American civil religion has been carefully defined, we proceed to develop propositions concerning the structure and functions of American civil religion. Chapter four explores the relationship between American civil religion and other institutions in American society. Coleman's (1970) evolutionary theory of civil religion is used as a point of reference. Coleman proposes that American civil religion is structurally differentiated from political and religious institutions, and that American civil religion performs specialized religious functions which are not performed by other institutions. Theoretical propositions and empirical support concerning the differentiation of American civil religion from denominationalism and politics are examined, and attempts are made to identify and specify the unique functions performed by American civil religion.

The final objective of the book is to explore the relationship between American civil religion and social change. Coleman (1970) proposes that the differentiation of American civil religion from politics and denominationalism follows the general direction of cultural evolution. Chapter five assesses evidence to determine whether civil religious patterns are consistent with the patterns of social change identified by sociological theories of religious evolution and secularization. Durkheimian and Parsonian evolutionary theories and Martin's theory of secularization are generally congruent with the conception of a structurally and functionally differentiated American civil religion, while modern privatism offers the least support for a differentiated American civil religion.

Chapter six suggests some cross-cultural applications of civil religion theory. This chapter is not intended to provide a comprehensive survey of the cross-cultural civil religion literature. The main objective is to highlight American civil religion by contrasting the American case with three other civil religious types suggested by Coleman (1970). Data from modern Great Britain and Restoration Japan illustrate undifferentiated forms of civil religion. Studies of the Soviet Union support the conception of civil religion as secular nationalism, and the American data point to a case of differentiated civil religion. Analysis of the four sample cases suggests that the type of civil religious development observable in a society is related to the level of differentiation within that society, in combination with the degree of historical toleration of religious pluralism.

The book concludes with the recommendation that further inquiry concerning American civil religion be guided by a set of three propositions adapted from Coleman's evolutionary elaboration of the transcendent universal model of American civil religion. The propositions provide a structure of orientation for the sociologist confronted with the labyrinth of civil religion literature, and a system of guidance for further scientific inquiry concerning American civil religion. The book in its entirety is conceived as a synthesis of American civil religion theory and research, intended as the first stage of an on-going process by which data on American civil religion are gathered, ordered, and formalized, for the eventual purpose of being tested against new data.

CHAPTER 2

THE INTELLECTUAL HISTORY OF CIVIL RELIGION

The intellectual development of the concept of American civil religion spans a variety of disciplines including philosophy, theology, history, and the social sciences. The works of almost any scholar interested in the nature of the church-state relationship could be viewed as relevant to the analysis of civil religion. It is therefore necessary to limit the intellectual history according to two criteria. First, this chapter will be confined to those studies selected from outside the sociological tradition, that have had the greatest impact upon the subsequent development of the sociological concept of American civil religion. The purpose is to examine the role of other disciplines in laying the foundation for the sociological perspective. Secondly, the primary focus of the intellectual history is upon studies that treat civil religion systematically, contribute basic definitions of civil religion, or generate assumptions about the institutionalization of civil religion in society.

Significant contributions to the study of American civil religion appear in the ideas of Rousseau, in the writings of Tocqueville and in the works of a collection of religious historians represented by the ideas of Hudson, Mead, and Marty. Rousseau provided the first definition of civil religion, and Tocqueville was the first to observe and systematically document civil religion in American society. The selected works of religious historians are concerned with identifying both the historical origins and modern religious implications of American civil religion. To assist analysis and comparison, each contribution to the American civil religion literature is classified as representative of one of the five models of American civil religion suggested by Richey and Jones (1974) and already outlined in Chapter 1.

A.   The Foundations: Rousseau and Tocqueville

The term civil religion first appears in Rousseau's *The Social Contract* (1893). While the relationships between religious and political ideas have been discussed throughout the history of social thought, Rousseau provides the first description of a belief system explicitly labeled civil religion. Rousseau's civil religion emerges in the context of his larger interest in legitimacy of the social bond. In a chapter entitled, "Of Civil Religion," which was added shortly before the publication of *The Social Contract,* Rousseau advocates a religion of civil virtue which would consecrate and legitimate common social life.

Rousseau arrives at the necessity for a civil religion after examining various ways that religion may function in relationship to the social order. Rousseau observes that throughout history, political institutions have depended upon religious legitimacy. Primitive societies were often theocracies, and monarchs claimed divine inspiration to strengthen collective loyalty. But the power of religious institutions and the divisiveness of religious sectarianism have ultimately proven threatening to political stability. Rousseau proposes that social cohesion could best be served by the requirement that the political leader establish a civil religion based on the dogmas of the existence of God, life after death, the reward of just behavior, the punishment of transgressions, and the sanctity of the social contract and the law (Rousseau, 1893/1913:121).

In the ideal society that Rousseau envisioned, civil religion would serve a dual function. Established by and under a political ruler, civil religion would legitimize the political order without establishing a competing religious authority. Civil religion, conceived by Rousseau as a state-directed religion of good citizenship, would perform the social functions of insuring political legitimacy and social cohesion. Although Rousseau's civil religion proclaims a belief in an omnipotent God,there is no evidence of a prophetic function. Rousseau's civil religion is ultimately a form of self-transcendent religious nationalism.

Alexis de Tocqueville's description of a "republican religion" in the nineteenth-century United States has been influential both for historians and sociologists of American civil religion. Tocqueville's view of civil religion differs significantly from that of his countryman Rousseau. Rousseau developed his conception of civil religion by abstractly considering the requirements of the ideal society. Tocqueville discovered republican religion during an empirical examination of American life in the 1830s. Rousseau wrote of a civil religion established by the state, while Tocqueville observed a form of civil religion that emerged precisely in the situation of church-state separation that Rousseau believed would undermine social cohesion. Both Rousseau and Tocqueville were motivated by an interest in the role of religious ideals in the European political future. Tocqueville's reliance on the American case as a predictive type established him as a forerunner of American historians and social scientists who would describe American civil religion as a folk religion of the American people (e.g. Herberg, 1955; Marty, 1959; Warner, 1961).

During Tocqueville's tour of America in 1831, he was impressed by the popularity of both religious values and democratic ideas. Focusing on the character and habits of the American populace, and relying on interviews and observation, Tocqueville constructed a model of a democratic and republican Christianity which functions as a nonsectarian folk religion. Republican religion is specifically the moral law which, through its influence on customs and domestic life, indirectly affects political life (Tocqueville, Vol. I, 1835/1966:304). The various American religious denominations might disagree about specific matters of denominational *doctrine,* but all agreed on general Christian *mores.*

Tocqueville presented a model of American civil religion in which religious belief and morality were fused with a political system of democratic values and laws. Such a fusion might generally imply the existence of a state church or a politically established belief system like that proposed by Rousseau. Instead, Tocqueville believed that the symbiotic relationship between American religious and political values was due particularly to the innovative American feature of legal nonestablishment. The separation of the denominations from political institutions left religion free to inform political decisions without being dependent upon the success or failure of a particular government. Tocqueville's republican religion was sufficiently nondenominational to act also as a generalized belief system which could bind divisions of religious and political loyalties. In Tocqueville's model, republican religion performed a socially integrating function as a mechanism for preventing liberty from degenerating into anarchy. By emphasizing the cohesive function of republican religion for American society, Tocqueville necessarily limited its prophetic potential. Tocqueville warned that republican religion was rooted in public opinion and could serve the conservative forces of the "tyranny of the majority" (Vol. II, 1835/1966:236).

Tocqueville's model of republican religion was the first description of a generalized democratic belief system based upon the religious and moral traditions of a society, which is observed to be structurally and functionally differentiated from both political and religious institutions. Republican religion appears to have been derived from the American denominations, but not to have been delimited by any particular church or sect. Republican religion supported a democratic political system but did so indirectly in infusing the folkways and mores of citizens. Democracy and equality were thus interpreted as political ideas with religious dimensions. Tocqueville hoped that republican religion could be generalizable to Europe. But, he also recognized the singularity of the American experience. Tocqueville's model of democratic and republican folk religion has had its greatest impact on American historical and social thought.

B. The Civil Religions of American Religious Historians

American religious historians have demonstrated considerable interest in the concept of civil religion. In a review of such literature, Phillip Hammond (1976:170) notes that Sydney E. Ahlstrom's 1,000 page volume, *A Religious History of the American People* (1972) focuses upon American civil religion as one of its major themes. Bedell, Sandon, and Wellborn's *Religion in America* (1975) also devotes considerable attention to the topic of American civil religion. Additionally, civil religion in America has been a subject of special concern for a number of American religious historians. Winthrop Hudson (1970) and other Protestant civic pietists locate the origin and boundaries of civil religion in the American Protestant tradition. Sidney Mead (1963; 1967) has devoted a considerable portion of his career to documenting the concept of a transcendent universal civil religion of the American nation. Other religious historians such as Martin Marty (1959; 1974) see American civil religion now becoming differentiated from its Protestant roots and developing into a generalized and secularized folk religion. Each of these differing but partially overlapping conceptions of civil religion among American religious historians has contributed significantly to the current status of American civil religion as a sociological concept.

1. The Origin of Protestant Civic Piety — Winthrop Hudson

Richey and Jones (1974:17-18) report that a particular view of American civil religion as a form of Protestant civic piety is found among the writings of James Smylie (1963), Winthrop Hudson (1970), Robert Michaelson (1970), and James Maclear (1971), among others. These scholars emphasize that the origins of American civil religion can be traced to a synthesis of American Protestantism and nationalism. Additional treatments of Protestant civic piety include H. Richard Niebuhr's (1937) discussion of the influences of Puritanism, Evangelicalism, and the Social Gospel on American civil beliefs, and Ernest Tuveson's (1968) study of the role of Protestant millennial themes in American history. The work of Winthrop Hudson may serve as representative of the Protestant civic piety model.

In his "Introduction" to *Nationalism and Religion in America* (1970), Winthrop Hudson attributes the origin of American civil religion to Protestant civic piety. Using historical data, he concludes that the American colonists were bound together by their common political and religious traditions. The common religious orientation was English Puritanism, and the dominant political view was a strong belief in the value of liberty (Hudson, 1970:xxv). The fusion of these traditions in America formed the basis for the new nation's civil religion.

There are two assumptions critical to Hudson's description of American Protestant civic piety. First, he assumes that British history embodied democratic values which were then expressed and experienced within the Puritan tradition. Second, he assumes that the American colonists experienced sufficient British identification to try to build a new Britain in the new world. According to Hudson (1970:xxxi), the American Revolution was conducted against a tarnished England in order to reestablish its original ideals in the colonies. Both assumptions are supported by Hudson's historical data. Of special interest to social scientists is the fact that Hudson describes an American civil religion derived from the values of a colonial culture which functioned as a mechanism for the social cohesion of the colonies.

Charles Long (1974:211-221) criticizes historians who, like Hudson, define American civil religion in the Protestant civic piety tradition. Long's main objection is that the narrow concept of Protestant civic piety contributes to the historical and cultural invisibility of such diverse American groups such as Native Americans, blacks, Catholics, and Jews. As Richey and Jones (1974:18) note, Protestant civic piety is the least comprehensive of the five models of American civil religion. The concept of Protestant civic piety, as used by Hudson and others, refers only to Protestant beliefs about the role of the American nation, rather than to a differentiated civil belief system available to all American citizens.

2.Sidney Mead's Transcendent Universal Religion of the Nation

Religious historian Sidney Mead (1963;1967; 1975) challenges the thesis that American civil religion can be narrowly defined as Protestant civic piety. Mead documents an American civil religion based on a synthesis of deistic and democratic principles, and characterized by a synergistic cosmopolitanism. Mead locates the origin of American civil religion in the Western European tradition by which emerging nations adapted the ideal of Christian universalism to their own nationalistic interests. The United States departed from the European pattern by separating church from state and refusing to establish any of the denominations. America became a nation based on the legitimacy of religious diversity (Mead, 1963). Mead would agree with the Protestant civic pietists that early American pluralism was dominated by the Protestant tradition. Mead (1963:135) believes, however, that by the second half of the nineteenth century America had "two religions," the Protestant orthodoxy of the denominations and a "religion of the Republic." The latter was the civil religion of a democratic society.

Mead (1967, 1975) describes the religion of the American republic that emerged under the structure of religious pluralism. Only within a pluralistic system, in which no denomination could be established, could the *nation itself* begin to fulfill the traditional religious functions of providing a major source of social cohesion, personal meaning and identity for citizens, and prophecy for historical roles. According to Mead, religious differentiation produced a differentiated and highly generalized religion of the Republic, partially separate from the denominations but also standing over them to insure against the self-transcendent and particularistic tendencies of the individual denominations. On the pluralistic international scene, the values of American civil religion could perform similar religious functions, and could serve as prophetic guidelines to world unity while guarding against the tendency toward nationalism. Mead is exceptional among American religious historians for tracing American civil religion from its Protestant origins beyond Protestant particularism and self-deifying nationalism to potentially universalistic application. The key to this logical progression is Mead's focus upon the unique social form of American religious pluralism in the generation of a divinely transcendent American civil religion.

3. The History of American Folk Religion: Martin Marty

In *The New Shape of American Religion* (1959) Martin Marty attempts to document the emergence of American civil religion as a fourth major American religion, independent and differentiated from Protestantism, Catholicism, and Judaism. Marty would agree with Mead that American civil religion was born in the natural religious beliefs of the nation's Protestant-deist founders, and has been nurtured by the American tradition of religious pluralism. Marty's position differs from both Mead and the Protestant civic pietists in its evaluation of American civil religion as a "religion-in-general" which lacks the moral and theological rigor of denominational religion. Marty's (1959:2) American "religion-in-general" is a syncretistic belief system in which generalized religious sentiments have replaced particularistic theological content. Franklin Littell (1962:162) presents a similar description of religion-in-general as the uncritical support of everything that is American, typified by the popular mass media slogan, "Go to the Church of Your Choice, but GO TO CHURCH!" The prophets of religion-in-general are popular American clergymen, such as the Rev. Billy Graham and Dr. Norman Vincent Peal, both of whom have attracted cross-denominational support. Religion-in-general is described by Marty as a popular, highly generalized symbol system concerned with the religious aspects of being an American. Similar to Marty's religion-in-general is Will Herberg's (1955, 1974) description of a religionized version of the American way of life, which provides a religiously pluralistic America with an overarching basis of unity. Marty, Littell, and Herberg portray American civil religion as a folk religion performing an integrating function for American society.

C. Conclusion

American religious historians were among the first to document the emergence of an American civil religion which overlapped with, but was also differentiated from, the denominations. For Hudson and the other Protestant civic pietists, America's civil religion was a nationalized version of Puritanism. The functions of Protestant civic piety were to foster cohesion by extending the Puritan covenant to the national level, and to provide prophetic guidance to a new nation under God. But the United States did not remain a totally Puritan, or even completely Protestant, nation. Mead was the first religious historian to recognize fully the impact of religious pluralism on American civil religion. As the American

9

religious structure became progressively differentiated and Protestant symbols became restricted in their applicability to the denominations, the symbols of American civil religion expanded to fill the void. Every American, Protestant or not, could potentially identify with the values of liberty and equality and believe in the divine guidance of a nation throughout history. Other scholars, such as Marty, Littell, and Herberg were concerned that the emerging values of American civil religion constituted a watered-down version of Protestantism which competed with the denominations in the field of religious meaning systems. In Marty's view, differentiation of religious structures has led to the generalization of civil religious values to the point where theological content is lost and national self-transcendence becomes the result. Marty, Mead, and the Protestant civic pietists agree on the existence of American civil religion and the manner of its emergence in American society. But, they disagree profoundly on its present form, functions, and depth. This same debate exists among contemporary sociologists of religion.

CHAPTER 3

THE SOCIOLOGICAL TRADITION

The civil religion debate among religious historians has its parallel among sociologists. Central to the debate within sociology is a controversy concerning the very definition of American civil religion. The initial section of this chapter highlights two prominent sociological models of American civil religion, W. Lloyd Warner's folk religion, and Robert Bellah's transcendent universal religion of the American nation. Since Bellah's model has been most influential for generating subsequent sociological inquiry, the response to Bellah, both theoretical and empirical, is briefly discussed. Bellah's model also provides the basis for a sociological definition of American civil religion which is framed to promote conceptual clarification of the American civil religion literature.

A. The Folk Religion of W. Lloyd Warner

The earliest sociological studies of American civil religion treated it as a folk religion emerging from the daily life-experiences and expressions of the American populace. According to Richey and Jones (1974:15), folk religion "emerges out of the ethos and history of the society" ultimately to become "an idolatrous faith competing with particularistic religions." Andrew Greeley (1972:173) defines folk religion as "the religion of comfort and reassurance; the religion of self-righteousness," which may be contrasted with American civil religion in its more noble, theoretical, "elite" form.

A classic sociological analysis of American civil rellligion as folk religion is found in W. Lloyd Warner's (1961) examination of the Memorial Day celebrations of a Massachusetts community in the late 1930s. Warner does not use the term "American civil religion" nor does he describe a normative, civil religious system. It is Warner's thesis that Memorial Day ceremonies function as rituals to ease the individual's anxieties about death, and to unify diverse segments of the communi-ty in a way that competing, particularistic, religious organizations are unable to accomplish. The basic symbolic themes of Memorial Day are the sacrifice of the soldier's life for his country and the obligation of the living also to sacrifice for the good of the society. The theme of individual sacrifice for the nation is sym-bolized in various rituals including the wearing of blood-red poppies and the par-ticipation in public parades to the cemeteries where the war dead are buried. Warner (1974:99) stresses the unifying function of these folk rituals.

Rather than positing an ideal system of American civil religion, Warner takes his data from the life of the American people. The indicators of Warner's folk religion are functioning sets of civic rituals which are socially integrating and identity-reinforcing. This 'ceremonial model" of American folk religion has been criticized by historian John F. Wilson (1974:126) for including too extensive a range of phenomena as indicators of American civil religion. Wilson concludes that Warner fails to differentiate criteria of civil religious symbolism from other forms of cultural symbolic behavior. Warner's greatest contribution to the study of American civil religion was the suggestion that a broad range of potential in-dicators of civil religion may be found in public ritual.

Conrad Cherry has adopted Warner's strategy of symbolic analysis of American folk religion. In "American Sacred Ceremonies" (1970), Cherry explores three historical examples of ceremonial occasions which serve the ritual expression of American civil religion. These are the funerals of national founders Thomas Jefferson and John Adams in 1826, and the funeral of Robert F. Kennedy in 1968. The three events are examples of what Warner (1974:109) called national "cults of the dead" in which the living and dead are united, the living are also united together, and all members of the society are united with God and his purpose for the nation. In contrast to Warner, who stressed the unifying functions of national sacred symbol systems, Cherry (1970:308) considers the dual potential of American civil religious symbolism to foster either unity or divisiveness.

Warner's symbolic study of civil religious rituals is a classic illustration of the sociological version of the folk religion model of American civil religion. The major contributions of Warner are the location of American civil religion in the national symbol systems and ritual celebrations of the American public, and the recognition that such symbols and ritual behaviors perform the religious function of uniting believers in a moral community. Warner's careful elaboration of American folk religion stimulated other sociologists to question whether folk religion was the only manifestation of American civil religion. Might American civil religion have an "elite" form as Greeley (1972) suggests? If American civil religion were to manifest the functions traditionally associated with religious systems, a prophetic dimension could be expected. Perhaps the greatest contribution of the folk religion tradition in sociology was the stimulus of further inquiry into the manifestations of American civil religion in American life.

B. The Transcendent Civil Religion of Robert Bellah

In 1967, sociologist Robert Bellah began to write of a transcendent, universal religion of the American nation. Transcendent universal religion consists of a set of divinely transcendent, normative ideals by which a society is defined, integrated, and ultimately judged (Richey and Jones, 1974:15-16). Transcendent universal religion differs from folk religion in two important respects. First, transcendent religion assumes a system of national ideals which exist as social facts apart from the extent of their acceptance by the American populace at any point in time. Folk religion, in contrast, takes the daily life behavior of the public as its major data source. Second, transcendent religion is seen as fulfilling all of the functions attributed to traditional religious systems. The functions of folk religion are limited to only two of the traditional social functions performed by religion, the creation and legitimation of cultural meaning and social integration. Transcendent universal religion is a civil religion capable of fulfilling the integrating and legitimizing functions of folk religion, with the additional function of divine prophetic guidance.

1. The Definition of Transcendent Universal American Civil Religion

In an article entitled "Civil Religion in America" (1967), Robert Bellah introduced the concept of transcendent universal religion of the nation into the realm of sociological discourse. Bellah's subsequent model of American civil religion flows from the Durkeimian assumption that social cohesion rests upon common moral understandings rooted in religious meaning structures (Bellah, 1975:ix). Bellah's model also is based on Parsons' (1966:10-11) theory of a religiously-based moral order (although Bellah does not necessarily accept all of Parsons' assumptions). Bellah asserts that American civil religion exists as a social fact, subject to the same type of inquiry as other religious systems. Bellah defines American civil religion as an institutionalized collection of sacred beliefs about the American nation (Bellah, 1967:8). The symbols of American civil religion and their institutionalization in American society may be observed through the systematic examination of national documents. Specifically, Bellah examines the Declaration of Independence and the inaugural addresses of American presidents as indicators of the beliefs and values of American civil religion. Central to the American civil belief system in the seventeenth and eighteenth centuries was a belief in the existence of God, in the American nation being subject to God's laws, and in the divine guidance and protection of the nation (Bellah, 1967:6). Common civil religious values were liberty, justice, charity, and personal virtue (Bellah, 19975:x). America was often characterized by its early citizens as a new Israel, a wilderness that could be revealed as a paradise for God's chosen people (Bellah, 1975:5-6). According to Bellah (1975:153), these historical American beliefs, values, and symbols have a sacred dimension because "they have revealed what reality is and how we should act in relation to it."

Although the symbols of American *civil* religion are often rich in biblical imagery, they are clearly differentiated from the symbols of American *denominational* religion. Bellah observes that from its inception, American civil religion did not oppose, and in fact shared much in common, with Christianity. Yet, American civil religion was not specifically sectarian or explicitly Christian. The differentiation of American civil religion from Christianity occurred early in American history because founders such as Franklin, Washington, and Jefferson determined that there should be a division of functions between the two types of religion (Bellah, 1967:8).

2. The History of American Civil Religion

In *The Broken Covenant: American Civil Religion in Time of Trial* (1975) Bellah traces the symbolic history of American civil religion from seventeenth century Puritanism through the mid-1970s. The unifying symbolism of the American "covenant" is conceived of as existing between God and the citizens of the society. The covenant symbolism of American civil religion emerged initially in the parallel religious and political ideologies of the New England Calvinists. The American Constitution was written by men who had experienced the climates of spiritual conversion and political revolution. The Constitution is an "external covenant" with a religious foundation, requiring periodic revival of its moral directive (Bellah, 1975:33-34). By conceiving of the United States Constitution as a type of covenant, Bellah provides an analogue for his model of American civil religion. The Constitution is clearly a political document guiding the political organization of a society. Yet, it also is based on the religious ideal of citizens bound to a higher moral order. The image of Constitution-as-covenant symbolizes the religious dimension of the American polity.

The concept of an American covenant is strongly suggestive of the unifying function of American civil religion. Bellah does not maintain that the potential for unity is always fulfilled. Instead, he observes that the new American covenant was violated in the genocide of the American Indians and in the institution of slavery. It required the revivalism of nineteenth-century evangelicalism and abolitionism, guided by the moral example of an Abraham Lincoln, to restore the covenant. Bellah views the twentieth century as a "new time of trial," as the American covenant is torn both internally and externally by two major sources of division, racial conflict and economic instability. Bellah's (1975) image of the "broken covenant" represents the contemporary state of a nation which is internally divided and out of touch with its transcendent values.

3. Conclusion

Bellah is the first to develop a sociological model of a transcendent universal American civil religion. According to John F. Wilson (1974:127-129), Bellah's model refers to several distinct dimensions and functions of American civil religion neglected by previous models. Wilson concludes that Bellah's model of American civil religion is superior to Warner's folk religion model. Although both include some of the same dimensions and sources of data, Bellah's model succeeds over Warner's in identifying specific types of civil religious behavior and belief. Bellah's model also contains a central element missing from folk religion, theology. The central, theological dimension of Bellah's American civil religion refers to a transcendent God. In contrast to the theologically weak folk religion model, Bellah stresses the transcendent and universal features of American civil religion which could make it, in Bellah's worlds, "simply one part of a new civil religion of the world" (Bellah, 1967:18). Of all of the elements of Bellah's model of Amerian civil religion, it is its theological dimension which has generated the greatest amount of subsequent controversy.

C. Responses to Bellah

The reaction to Bellah's sociological model of a transcendent universal American civil religion was considerable. Several books (e.g., Cherry, 1971; Novak, 1974; Richey and Jones, 1974) and numerous articles (e.g., Cherry, 1970; Coleman, 1970; Fenn, 1972, 1974, 1976; Greeley, 1972: Chap. 7; Jolicoeur and Knowles, 1978; Neuhaus, 1970, Stauffer, 1973; Thomas and Flippen, 1972; Wimberley, 1976) appeared in direct or indirect response to Bellah's model. Contemporary social scientists were not responding simply to the concept of American civil religion. Historical models (e.g., Tocqueville, 1835; Hudson, 1970; Marty, 1959; Mead, 1967) have been well-known but have stimulated little sociological attention. Warner's folk religion model had become a sociological classic, but generated only sporadic sociological inquiry in the 1970s (e.g., Cherry, 1970; Greeley, 1972). Bellah renewed intellectual inquiry into American civil religion by seriously postulating the existence of a transcendent universal American civil religion, which, in its impact on American culture, went far beyond ceremonial occasions. Bellah also suggested a systematic method for the study of American civil religion through the examination of national documents. Bellah's model and his methods stimulated two types of response, theoretical and empirical. Theoretical statements by Fenn (1976) and Greeley (1972) are representative of the theoretical evaluations of Bellah's model. Relevant empirical tests include published studies by Jolicoeur and Knowles (1978), Thomas and Flippen (1972) and Wimberley (1976). This chapter includes only a brief overview of selected examples of the theoretical and empirical response to Bellah's model. In chapter four, Fenn's response and the empirical studies are examined in greater detail as sources for the generation of theoretical propositions concerning American civil religion.

1. Theoretical Response

a. Richard Fenn

Bellah's most outspoken critic has been Richard Fenn (1972; 1974; 1976; 1978). While Fenn is skeptical of Bellah's entire American civil religion model, the heart of his critique is his disagreement with Bellah's assumptions concerning the function of religion in contemporary American society. At the center of the controversy between Bellah and Fenn are questions concerning the existence of a common culture in the United States and the ability of religion to provide the basis for such a social integration. Both Bellah and Fenn ask the following questions, but arrive at different conclusions. (1) Does American society exist as an ideological whole? (2) Can religion provide moral integration for modern society? (3) Does American civil religion exist as a social fact of contemporary life? (4) Can civil religion provide a basis for twentieth-century ideological renewal? and (5) Is it a proper role for the scientific observer to call for a reaffirmtion of civil faith in a morally torn society? Bellah's model is based on an affirmative response to all five questions, while Fenn's critique is based on a negative response.

Fenn questions Bellah's basic premise that American civil religion exists as a social fact institutionalized in the American social structure. He (1976:165) grants the possibility that American civil religion could have provided an overarching value system in the early history of the society, but believes that American civil religious symbolism fails to bind cultural, social, and personal spheres of action in contemporary secularized America.

b. Andrew Greeley

Greeley devotes a chapter of The Denominational Society (1972:156-174) to "The Civil Religion." Unlike Fenn, Greeley has no problem conceiving of an overarching normative order in American society. "The sociologist, accustomed as he is from reading Durkheim and Weber to expect religion in society, is not terribly surprised by these sacral underpinnings of the American consensus" (Greeley, 1972:157). After reviewing the folk religion models of Eckhardt (1958), Herberg (1955), and Marty (1959), Greeley concludes that there is more to the American normative consensus than a watered-down religion in general. Folk religion is only one observable manifestation of American civil religion. The other manifestation is the noble, prophetic elite form of American civil religion. Greeley concurs with Bellah's location of the symbols of American civil religion in national documents and civic celebrations. Greeley also agrees that the symbols of American civil religion reveal that the American nation has a religious dimension represented, in part, by the celebration of sacred places and sacred days. Like Bellah, Greeley finds no contradiction in the possibility that folk and elite forms of civil religion could exist alongside of one another in the same society.

2. Empirical Response

a. Thomas and Flippen

Only a few empirical studies have specifically investigated transcendent civil religion in America. Thomas and Flippen's (1972) content analysis of the editorials of a national sample of newspapers published during the "Honor America" weekend, July 4, 1970, is one of the earliest empirical responses to Bellah's model. The purpose of the study was a specific test of Bellah's thesis of a universal transcendent civil religion in American society. Analysis of data indicated that a fairly large number of secular civil themes were found in the Honor America editorials, but few of the themes specifically referred to a diety. Thomas and Flippen (1972:224) conclude that, although many of the values Bellah attributes to American civil religion are significant values of American culture, these values are *not commonly attributed to divine origin,* and are therefore not representatitive of a transcendent civil religion.

b. Jolicoeur and Knowles

Another content analysis, using a different measurement instrument than that used by Thomas and Flippen, reports evidence of transcendent civil religious beliefs among Masonic fraternal orders. Jolicoeur and Knowles (1978) found a high proportion of civil religious statements in issues of a national Masonic journal, *The New Age.* Jolicoeur and Knowles interpret their findings as supportive of Bellah's model of transcendent universal American civil religion.

c. Ronald C. Wimberley

Numerous surveys conducted by Ronald C. Wimberley and his colleagues (e.g., Wimberley et al., 1976; Wimberley, 1976; Christenson and Wimberley, 1978; Wimberley, 1979; Wimberley, 1980; Wimberley and Christenson, 1980) were designed to test Bellah's model of transcendent universal American civil religion at the level of individual belief. Because the surveys relied on similar and consistent civil religion measurement items (see appendix), the surveys are treated collectively here, with specific conclusions of some of the studies cited in more detail in chapter four.

Factor and cluster analysis of data from two of the earlier studies (Wimberley et al., 1976; Wimberley, 1976) revealed a separate civil religious dimension of individual belief which was distinct from indicators of both denominational religious belief and political commitment. Regression analysis of data from the second survey (Wimberley, 1980:44) found an association between civil religious belief and support for Richard Nixon in the 1972 Presidential election. In most cases, civil religious orientation predicted political choice with greater precision than other variables, including denominational religious belief, socioeconomic status, and most measures of political orientation. Data from a more extensive state-wide survey (Christenson and Wimberley, 1978:78:80) confirmed that the level of civil religious orientation was higher among political and religious conservatives, but that civil religious tenets have a rather broad support among the majority of Americans. Wimberley and Christenson conclude that their findings provide support for Bellah's transcendent universal civil religion model at the individual level of analysis (Christenson and Wimberley, 1978:80).

3. Conclusion

The response to Bellah has been immediate and mixed. On the theoretical front Richard Fenn emerges as Bellah's most adamant and sophisticated antagonist. Fenn doubts the very existence of American civil religion and is particularly skeptical of Bellah's transcendent model of American civil religion. In contrast, Greeley is comfortable with the idea of an overarching belief system for society, and finds Bellah's model to be a productive analysis of civil religion in its elite form. The theoretical state of American civil religion within contemporary sociology has become an ongoing pro-Bellah versus anti-Bellah debate. Other voices in the next round of the debate will be heard in the following chapters as the issue of theoretical clarification is addressed.

The empirical responses to Bellah's model are still in their infancy. Studies attempting to determine if American civil religion exists are hampered by the absence of a clear definition of American civil religion which is universally accepted in the social sciences. Different studies use different civil religion measurement instruments, making comparison of results extremely difficult. The methodological problems of American civil religion measurement are embedded in the current chaos of American civil religion theory. Until a logical, coherent model of American civil religion can be systematized in the form of testable propositions, American civil religion is likely to remain elusive to empirical investigators.

D. An Emerging Definition

The analysis of differing traditions of research and differing theoretical models of American civil religion demonstrates the need for conceptual clarification. Much of the confusion can be traced to the coexistence in the literature of the five models of American civil religion; folk religion, democratic faith, religious nationalism, Protestant civic piety, and transcendent universal religion of the nation (Richey and Jones, 1974). The five models have different emphases, but are also interconnected at various points. In order to simplify the complexity and move American civil religion research out of its pioneering stage, selection of the most productive model or synthesis of models is in order. Because the transcendent universal model of Robert Bellah is the most comprehensive and has been the most empirically productive of the five models, it will serve as the basic model from which both a definition and some assumptions concerning American civil religion will be derived.

The transcendent universal American civil religion of Bellah (1967, 1975) is the most comprehensive of the five models, due to the fact that it includes the other four models as possible manifestations of the basic model or as departures from it. Bellah (1975), who placed the origins of American civil religion within the American Puritan tradition, includes the Protestant civic piety model as typical of early American civil religion. Bellah would argue, however, that Protestant values have to be universalized and generalized to integrate diverse groups into the American tradition. The 1961 inaugural speech of President John F. Kennedy, a Roman Catholic, illustrates the success of the generalization of values (Bellah, 1967:5). The transcendent universal model also contains options for the expression of folk religion and religious nationalism. Through the image of the "broken covenant" Bellah (1975) symbolizes the idolatrous application of American civil values to public theology and national self-worship. Bellah does not directly address the democratic faith model of personal value construction. But, Bellah himself exemplifies individual adherence to a humanistic (and in Bellah's case, theological) belief system shaped by the values of American civil religion. The transcendent universal model advanced by Bellah is the most inclusive of the five models because, by describing American civil religion in its ideal, normative form, all civil religious behavior directed toward or away from the ideal can be measured and included for analysis. As has been previously noted, the transcendent universal model of Bellah has stimulated more recent sociological empirical studies (e.g., Jolicoeur and Knowles, 1978; Thomas and Flippen, 1972; Wimberley et al., 1976; Wimberley, 1976; Wimberley and Christenson, 1980) than have alternative models.

One of the limitations of Bellah's model has been the absence of a precise definition of American civil religion which distinguishes American civil religion from *other* religious forms and from civil *society*. Bellah originally defines American civil religion as an institutionalized collection of sacred beliefs, symbols, and rituals, constituting "a religious dimension for the whole fabric of American life, including the political sphere" (Bellah, 1967:3-4). John A. Coleman (1970), working with the transcendent universal model, has derived a more specific definition of American civil religion. Coleman suggests that a definition of *civil* religion should be a logical outgrowth of a definition of religion. Coleman (1970:68) follows Bellah's (1964:171) definition of religious as "a set of symbolic acts which relate man to the ultimate conditions of his existence." Using Bellah's definition of religion and its functions, and applying these to the society and the citizens's role, Coleman develops the most precise definition of civil religion to emerge from the literature. Coleman's (1970:69) definition of civil religion, which has been condensed and slightly reworded to apply to *American* civil religion, states that *America civil religion is the religious symbol system which relates the citizen's role and American society's place in space, time, and history to the conditions of ultimate existence and meaning.* Coleman's definition, is a logical outgrowth of Bellah's sociology of religion and Bellah's transcendent universal model of American civil religion. In his 1975 work, Bellah offers a similar definition, calling civil religion "that religious dimension, found. . .in the life of every people, through which it interprets its historical experience in the light of transcendent reality" (Bellah, 1975:3). Coleman's definition has the advantage of including reference to both the individual and societal levels of civil religion.

The fact that there has been no single, agreed-upon definition of American civil religion hinders the development of a coherent body of knowledge in the field. Currently, different theorists and researchers rely on differing, and occasionally conflicting definitions of American civil religion, making comparison of studies difficult. Coleman's definition of American civil religion is cited here as an aid to conceptual synthesis. Coleman's definition offers a succinct statement of transcendent universal religion of the nation without excluding the other four models of American civil religion (Richey and Jones, 1974). Each of the prevailing models of American civil religion can be treated as sub-types, or variations, within the general framework of Coleman's definition. Coleman's definition of American civil religion is the basic definition used through the remainder of this book because it is the most precise, synthetic definition to emerge from the sociological literature. In the following chapters we rely on Coleman's definition as the foundation for three propositions which are intended to clarify civil religion theory.

CHAPTER 4

THEORETICAL PROPOSITIONS AND EMPIRICAL SUPPORT

*A. The Differentiation of Civil Religion from American
Denominationalism and Politics*

Phillip Hammond's (1976) bibilographic essay on the sociology of American civil religion organizes the civil religion literature around five central questions. The first, and most frequently posed question, "What *is* the American civil religion?" (Hammond, 1976:171), has been answered in the preceding chapter. American civil religion has been defined as the religious symbol system that relates the citizen's role and American society's place in space, time, and history to the conditions of ultimate existence and meaning (Coleman, 1970:69). Based on this definition, further sociological questions may now be addressed. Two other substantive questions raised by Hammond (1976:171) are "What has been the *course* of American civil religion?" and "What is the *relationship* between American civil religion and churches?" Both questions may be addressed by first tracing the history of American civil religion from its origin to contemporary times. It will be shown that Parsons (1971), Bellah (1964), Fenn (1970, 1976), Coleman (1970) and Cherry (1971) agree that the process of differentiation has had a pronounced impact on American religious symbol systems (although there is some disagreement about the precise results of the impact). Bellah's and Fenn's typologies of civil religion are juxtaposed to illustrate points of contention and consensus concerning the precise effect of differentiation upon American civil religion. There is general agreement in the theoretical literature that differentiation alters the relationship of American civil religion to other American institutions. Representative empirical studies are assessed for evidence concerning the current degree of differentiation between American civil religion and American denominations and politics. The discussion concludes with a proposition designed to guide further research concerning the effects of differentiation on American civil religion.

1. Theoretical Studies

a. Talcott Parsons

Determination of the level of differentiation of American civil religion from other social institutions is partially dependent upon the criterion of differentiation. Parsons (1971:26) defines differentiation as the process by which units in a social system divide into two or more parts functionally different from the original structure. In the general action system, differentiation may occur within systems or between major system levels. Types of differentiation relevant to the discussion of religious symbol systems include differentiation within the cultural system, within the social structure, between social and cultural systems, and between social and personality systems. Differentiation within the general religio-cultural system can take place. For example, particularistic values, such as religious fundamentalism, may arise to counteract the differentiation of more universal value systems. Differentiation within the cultural system may account for the differentiation of particularistic American public theology from the more transcendent universal values of Bellah's model of American civil religion. The separation of religious and political institutions in historic times serves as an example of differentiation within the social structure. The further differentiation of a civil religious structure, not dependent on the denominations or political institutions, would be an extension of this type of differentiation. Differentiation between system levels occurs because the two systems do not exactly overlap. The develoment of denominational pluralism in the United States is an example of congruent differentiation from the cultural system of Judeo-Christian values. Differentiation between social and personality systems would be evidenced when religious institutions are challenged by individual autonomy.

In the Parsonian model, three other processes of structural change accompany differentiation, adaptive upgrading, inclusion, and value generalization. Parsons (1971:26) specifies that differentiation at any level results in higher evolution if, and only if, each new unit has greater adaptive capacity than the old, previously undifferentiated unit. Parsons calls this process adaptive upgrading. With adaptive upgrading a wider range of resources becomes available to differentiating units than had been available to their predecessors. Both the processes of differentiation and adaptive upgrading pose problems for the integration of new units. The problems can be solved by the inclusion of the newly differentiated units within the normative structure of the society. Ultimately, the processes of differentiation, adaptive upgrading and inclusion are completed by value generalization. If newly differentiated units are to gain legitimacy in the increasingly complex social structure, value systems must be expressed at a higher level of generality in order to prevent social disorganization, (Parsons, 1971:27). The relationship between differentiation, adaptive upgrading, inclusion, and value generalization as outlined by Parsons is important for tracing the development of American civil religion. The transcendent universal model portrays an American civil religion which is differentiated from other social institutions, yet is sufficiently generalized to overarch and integrate these institutions during times of national crisis.

b. Robert Bellah

1. Theory of Religious Differentiation: Using a definition of differentiation similar to that of Parsons, Robert Bellah (1964) has developed a theory of religious evolution based on differentiation. Bellah traces the course of religious change through five ideal typical historical stages: (1) primitive religion (primarily Australian religions); (2) archaic religion (religions of Africa, Polynesia, and early religions of the Middle East and China); (3) historic religion (transcendental religion including Judaism, Islam and early Christianity); (4) early modern religion (the Protestant Reformation); and (5) modern religion (post-Reformation religions in Western nations). The major evolutionary process Bellah specifies is differentiation. Through the five successive stages, the evolution of religious symbol systems moves from compact to differentiated forms, the self becomes differentiated from the world, and religious institutions become differentiated from other institutions (Bellah, 1964:358). Bellah's five stages and the indicators of differentiaton for each stage are summarized in figure 1.

Figure 1. Bellah's Stages of Religious Evolution (Bellah, 1964)

INDICATORS OF DIFFERENTIATION	RELIGIOUS STAGE		
	PRIMITIVE (Most examples drawn from Australian religion)	ARCHAIC (Religions of Africa, Polynesia, and early religions of middle East, India, and China)	HISTORIC (Transcendental religions— Islam, Judaism, etc. Christianity, etc.)
Religious Organization	No religious organization exists apart from society	Emergence of the cult	Emergence of differentiated religious collectivities, including church-state differentiation
Religious Symbol Systems	Monistic — religious myths overlap significantly with daily life activity	The beginnings of dualism in the objectification of mythic beings	Dualistic — natural and supernatural worlds are separated
Self-World Relationship	Fusion of self with myth in ritual	Increased distinction between humans and gods	Clearly structured self-concept emerges to face transcendent reality

INDICATORS OF DIFFERENTIATION	RELIGIOUS STAGE	
	EARLY MODERN (Protestant Reformation)	MODERN (Post-Reformation religion in Western nations)
Religious Organization	Rejection of religious hierarchy (papal authority) and establishment of a "religious two class system: elect and reprobates" (369)	Denominational pluralism and privatization of religion
Religious Symbol Systems	Focus upon the direct relationship between the individual and transcendent reality	Multiple symbol systems open to individual selection
Self-World Relationship	This-worldly orientation of self-involvement	Multi-dimensional self, conceived of as capable of transforming both self and world

23

Although Bellah does not mention American civil religion in his general treatment of religious evolution, he makes several observations which can aid the construction of a theory of the dfferentiation of American civil religion. Bellah sets the stage of original church-state differentiation in the period of historic religion. Prior to this stage, religious and political institutions were not clearly differentiated. The Protestant Reformation of the early modern period initiated the uneasy religious pluralism of Europe which partially motivated American settlement by members of Protestant sects. At the same time that this structural differentiation of religious institutions was occuring, religious symbol systems were multiplying. According to Bellah, modern religion represents a distinctive evolutionary state in which traditional religious worldviews were challenged, first by the rational ethics of Kant and later by humanism. Bellah views this process as one of evolution from primitive monism, through historical dualism, to a modern structure of infinite possibilities. The modern effects of differentiation include moral erosion, yet, in Bellah's view, there are also expanded opportunities for innovation (Bellah, 1964:373-374). One such religious innovation which is congruent with the differentiation of religious organizations and symbol systems is the emergence of a differentiated American civil religion. Commenting on his system of religious evolution in a subsequent work, Bellah (1980:xi) points to the early modern and modern periods as the epochs most likely to produce a civil religion which is differentiated from both religious and political institutions.

2. *Bellah's Typology of American Civil Religion; General and Special Civil Religion:* Bellah is able to discern numerous dimensions and manifestations of American civil religion. Two manifestations, *general* and *special* civil religion, illustrate the effects of differentiation upon cultural values pertaining to civil religion. General civil religion, based on universal values, is the type of civil religion considered for many centuries to be a necessary prerequisite for political and social order. General civil religion provides the type of religious discipline necessary as the basis for the responsible, moral citizenship that leads to an integrated society (Bellah, 1976a:156). Tocqueville's (1835) concept of republican religion is a comprehensive classical analysis of general civil religion. Through republican religion's generalized synthesis of democratic values, and belief in a supreme being, a foundation of good citizenship and social cohesion is built.

In the United States a *special* form of civil religion developed which is congruent with, but partially differentiated from, the general values of the culture. In the case of the United States, special civil religion came to be based particularly upon the specific democratic values derived from the Declaration of Independence and the Revolutionary tradition (Bellah, 1976a:156). For example, the general belief in democratic values exemplifies general civil religion, while the derivation of these beliefs from the American Constitution illustrates special civil religion. Special civil religion is also evidenced in the belief in America as a "new Israel" (Bellah, 1976b:167). Bellah (1976a:156) notes the partial overlapping of general and special civil religion in American society, and observes that most religious groups in the United States have been able to affirm aspects of both general and special civil religion. Figure 2 illustrates the central attributes of general and special civil religion, presented here as varying along the Parsonian continuum of value generalization, which Parsons (1966:23) classifies as a process of modernization accompanying differentiation. Bellah's typology of general and special civil religion is more descriptive than predictive. Bellah suggests that forms of civil religion may vary in generality, ranging from the universal general civil religion to the particular special civil religion, but fails to specify the conditions under which special civil religion develops as a religious form which is partially differentiated from general civil religion. Bellah's typology remains a categorical tool most useful for describing different levels of value generalization observable in civil religious symbol systems.

c. Richard Fenn

Richard Fenn's (1976;1978) analysis of the effect of differentiation on civil religion differs substantially from the conclusions of Parsons and Bellah. Fenn views modern society as structurally differentiated beyond the capacities of religious systems to offer any overarching normative basis for integration. Fenn (1970:135) proposes that American society is highly differentiated *within* the cultural and structural systems and *between* the two system levels. Religious and ideological pluralism have replaced the unified, religiously-based moral order characteristic of less differentiated societies. Competing pluralistic systems of meaning are institutionalized in the society and internalized by individuals, providing a basis of contemporary ideological conflict.

Figure 2
Generality of Civil Religious Values (Bellah, 1976a)

Value Generalization

Universalism————————————————————————————————*Particularism*

I General Civil religion	*II Special Civil Religion*
Provides general moral basis for citizenship	provides specific national symbols of divine transcendence

In response to Bellah's typology Fenn (1976) has developed a typology of American civil religion which illustrates his own differentiation thesis. Fenn's two categories of American civil religion are produced by differentiation within religious culture. Fenn (1976:162) proposes that structural differentiation within modern society will increase the degree of separation between forms of religious culture. This phenomenon is illustrated by the emergence of two types of American civil religion which may be designated as *societal* and *personal* civil religion (See Bellah, 1976a:155). Societal civil religion combines national and biblical symbols and provides the motivational base of corporate actors within the social system. Personal civil religion expresses ethical piety and assists the identity development of individuals (Fenn, 1976:162). Figure 3 summarizes his typology. Fenn (1976:162) sees societal civil religion as comparable to Bellah's *special* civil religion, while personal civil religion is analogous to Bellah's *general* civil religion (see figure 2). Fenn argues that the differentiation of forms of American civil religion at the societal and individual levels is evidence that there is no overarching form of American civil religion that can bind the individual to society. In Fenn's view, American religious culture currently has no macro-level function, although values are manifestly important to the individual's personality. Applying this analysis to the religious dimension of the nation, Fenn (1976:165) concludes that societal civil religion (Bellah's special civil religion) has lost its function for contemporary society.

Figure 3

Personal and Societal Civil Religion (Fenn, 1976)

Differentiation within Religious Culture

Personality _____ *Social*
System   *System*

I Personal Civil Religion	*II Societal Civil Religion*
A. Provides for time- less identity	A. Provides socio- historical identity
B. Motivates individ- ual identity devel- opment	B. Motivates corporate actors

A comparison of the Fenn and Bellah typologies is made difficult by the fact that Fenn's categories of societal and personal civil religion are based on *structural* differentiation, while Bellah's types of special and general civil religion vary along a continuum of cultural *value* generalization. Value generalization and structural differentiation are complementary, but not identical, processes (Parsons, 1971:26-27). Fenn's conclusion that societal civil religion is exactly what Bellah means by special civil religion is questionable. Figure 4 presents the two typologies as if, as Fenn concludes, they were structurally parallel. According to figure 4, Bellah's special civil religion becomes progressively weakened in its ability to unite citizens with differing personal value systems. However, it is possible to agree with Fenn's differentiation thesis without accepting the assumption that special civil religion has lost its unifying potential. Figure 5 accounts for the possibility that elements of both general and special civil religion could be present at the societal level. Although societal and personal types of civil religion may be differentiated, as Fenn observes, both types may be subsumed under Bellah's category of special civil religion. Neither Bellah nor Fenn currently take the synthetic perspective suggested by figure 5, although this perspective is as logically possible as either of the independent typologies. Until there is further systematic development of both typologies and further specification of the factors assumed to produce typological variation, neither Bellah's nor Fenn's typology of American civil religion is likely to generate productive empirical research.

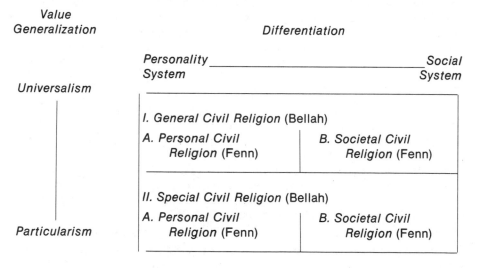

Figure 4
Bellah's versus Fenn's Typology of Civil Religion: Parrallel Perspective (Fenn, 1976)

Differentiation

Personality _____ *Social*
System   *System*

| I General Civil religion (Bellah) | II Special Civil Religion (Bellah) |
| I. Personal Civil Religion (Fenn) | II. Societal Civil Religion (Fenn) |

Figure 5
Bellah's versus Fenn's Typology of Civil Religion: Synthetic Perspective

Value
Generalization   *Differentiation*

Universalism

Particularism

Personality _____ *Social*
System   *System*

I. General Civil Religion (Bellah)	
A. Personal Civil Religion (Fenn)	B. Societal Civil Religion (Fenn)
II. Special Civil Religion (Bellah)	
A. Personal Civil Religion (Fenn)	B. Societal Civil Religion (Fenn)

d.   John A. Coleman

John A. Coleman (1970) proposes a theory of the structural differentiation of American civil religion that is logically consistent with the assumptions of both Parsons (1971) and Bellah (1964) concerning the differentiation of religious symbol systems. Coleman draws upon Bellah's (1964) religious evolutionary stages to illustrate the differentiation of contemporary civil religion from both religious and political institutions. It is Coleman's thesis, borrowed from Bellah (1967), that civil religion is "the essential middle term" necessary for understanding church-state differentiation (Coleman, 1970:68). In the stages of primitive and archaic religions, society, religion, and civil religion are observed to be *un*differentiated. In historic or early modern religious systems, church-state separation begins. Although political and religious organizations become differentiated, often posing conflicts of interest, forms of civil religion are not yet differentiated. Civil religion may be controlled either by religious institutions or by the state. In modern societies, civil religion may be observed in one of three forms. These are, (1) continuing to be undifferentiated, and sponsored by either religion or the state; (2) holding monopoly status as a form of secular nationalism; or (3) differentiated civil religion controlled neither by religion nor the state (Coleman, 1970:69).

Type 1, Continued undifferentiated civil religion: Coleman suggests that just because civil religion appears to be undifferentiated within a society, its absence should not be assumed. In these cases, civil religious functions will be performed either by religious or political institutions. Civil religion will appear either as church-sponsored or state-sponsored (Coleman, 1970:70).

In cases where an established religious tradition provides the context for sacred civic symbols, civil religion may be viewed as church-sponsored. The Christian-sponsored divine right of kings exemplifies church-sponsored civil religion. Modern examples of church-sponsorship in the Judaic and Islamic traditions include modern Israel and the Khomeini government of Iran. In such cases a differentiated civil religion is not discernible because political and religious symbol systems are intertwined under the sponsorship of a dominant religious tradition. State-sponsored civil religion, exemplified by Imperial Rome and Restoration Japan, is evidenced in cases where the political sytem institutes a nationally self-transcendent cult. Structural weaknesses of state-sponsored civil religion, observable in the Roman and Japanese cases, include the problem of value specificity which challenges the values of competing religious organizations (Coleman, 1970:72).

Type 2, Secular nationalism: Coleman views secular nationalism as a functional alternative to civil religion to the extent that secular nationalism provides a legitimating symbol system which competes with the symbol systems of religious organizations. The secular nationalism of the U.S.S.R. is a prime example. Other examples include Turkey after Ataturk's revolution and the Third Republic of France. The strains inherent in secular nationalism as a replacement for civil religion include persecution of religious citizens and limitations on religious and civil liberties (Colemen, 1970:72).

Type 3, Differentiated civil religion: Coleman relies directly on Bellah's evolutionary assumptions to predict the emergence of a differentiated form of civil religion in the most institutionally differentiated societies. The United States is such a differentiated society characterized both by church-state separation and religious pluralism. The differentiation of these structures makes religious or state domination of civil religion virtually impossible. If Sidney Mead (1967) is correct in his description of the transcendent quality of the traditional American conception of civil faith, then secular nationalism is also an unlikely choice for the United States. Thus, Coleman concludes that the United States is characterized by "almost a unique case" of differentiated civil religion (Coleman, 1970:74).

e. Conrad Cherry

Conrad Cherry (1971:15) believes that the differentiation of American civil religion from the American denominations is a recent, mid-twentieth century development. During the early history of the nation, and continuing into the twentieth century, the values of American civil religion were usually expressed in Protestant terms by Protestant spokesmen, resulting in a Protestant civic piety. But the American tradition of religious pluralism, advocated by most of the Protestant denominations, opened the way for the differentiation of alternative religious systems. Cherry believes that the increase in non-Protestant immigration and the fairly recent ascendancy of non-Protestants to positions of national power mark the point of differentiation of American civil religion from Protestant civic piety.

Perhaps as a by-product of its differentiated status, American civil religion has existed "in a relationship of tension" to some other American religions (Cherry, 1971:16). A major example of this relationship of tension is found in the rejection of civil religion's symbols and ceremonies by sects such as the Jehovah's Witnesses, whose members refuse to salute the American flag or pledge alllegiance to the nation. Martin and Peterson (1978) find, for example, that members of American sects such as the Assembly of God, Seventh Day Adventists, and Jehovah's Witnesses display lower levels of civil religiosity, as measured by opinion items than members of more established deominations. Members of these sects reject American civil religion as a religious option, and the values of American civil religion are not sufficiently general to avoid conflict with the sectarian values of these particular organizations. The very generalization of values, a process Parsons (1971) observes as accompanying the differentiation of a new social form, has been a source of conflict between American civil religion and traditional American denominations. Articulate American churchmen such as Marty (1959) have condemned American civil religion as an "American Shinto," or at best as a watered-down religion-in-general. The degree to which American churchmen have perceived civil religion as a threat to traditional religion is an indicator of the degree to which Amercan civil religion has become differentiated as a separate, potentially competing, religious system in American society.

2. Empirical Studies

a. Samuel Mueller and Paul Sites

An empirical study by Samuel Mueller and Paul Sites (1977) provides relevant data concerning the contemporary relationship between American civil religion and the American denominations. These data consist of tape recordings of religious services from a simple random sample of one-third of all churches in a metropolitan area of 500,000 (Akron, Ohio). The religious services were recorded on Sunday, July 4, 1976, the day of the American Bicentennial celebration. Analysis of data revealed that fifty-seven out of sixty Bicentennial services contained mention of the relationship between America's role in history and the conditions of ultimate reality.

The symbols and themes of American civil religion appeared equally in sermons given across all churches in the sample, including Protestant and Catholic churches, black and white churches, and among ethnic churches. Some denominational differences were observed, but no denomination strayed beyond the core set of civil religious values as defined by Bellah (1975). Because denominational and ethnic differences were not substantial, Mueller and Sites (1977:11) conclude that their data offers limited support for Bellah's thesis that

American civil religion exists, and that American civil religion transcends specific religious denominations.

How are Mueller and Site's findings to be interpreted with regard to Coleman's hypothesis that American civil religion is structurally differentiated from religious institutions? If the denominations espouse the values of American civil religion, can religious and civil religious systems be seen as differentiated? Careful examination of the data reveals that the values of Amercan civil religion and denominational values expressed in the sample sermons are held at different levels of generality. Mueller and Site's findings are consistent with Parsons' (1971) theory of the congruence of differentiation and value generalization. Mueller and Sites found evidence of civil religious values differentiated from denominational theology, yet couched at a sufficiently high level of generality to overarch denominational differences. These findings also support Coleman's structural differentiation hypothesis. When the values of American civil religion are found to be manifest at a high enough level of generality within institutions with more particularistic value systems, it can be assumed that denominational and civil religious values are differentiated from one another even though the two sets of values may at the same time be generally congruent. This combination allows for an American civil religion which is differentiated from the particularism of denominational theology, yet is sufficiently universal to overarch and integrate these institutions at the societal level.

b. Ronald C. Wimberley

A body of empirical research conducted by Ronald Wimberley and his colleagues lends support to the thesis that American civil religion is differentiated from both denominationalism and political commitment at the individual level of analysis. Two early studies (Wimberley et al., 1976; Wimberley, 1976) were based on separate surveys of individual religious, political, and civil religious beliefs. A factor analysis of data taken from the first survey, which did not include a measure of political belief, revealed four distinct first order factors, civil religion, religious belief, religious behavior, and religious experience. Second order factoring revealed that, while the civil religion dimension was positively correlated with several first order dimensions of denominational religiosity, the civil religious dimension remained distinct. Wimberley's second sample, which was larger and more religiously heterogeneous than the first, was surveyed on items of political belief, as well as religious and civil religious belief. Factoring of the religious and civil religious items confirmed the findings of the first study, although higher order analyses indicated that the religious and civil religious dimensions were more closely associated in the second sample than in the first (Wimberley, 1976:345). Factor analysis of the second survey also revealed that civil religion items factored distinctly away from political items. Second order analysis found that civil religion and political belief stayed together on one factor, and away from other political items (public behavior, social interaction, experience, private behavior, and political knowledge) (Wimberley, 1976:346-347). Thus, Wimberley found the civil religious dimension to be differentiated from both the religious and political dimensions of individual belief, as measured by the survey items. (See appendix for examples of Wimberley's civil religion measurement items).

A study by Wimberley and Christenson (1980), based on state survey data drawn from a sample of over 3000 respondents, explored the relationship between individual civil religious commitment and commitment to the principle of church-state separation. Wimberley and Christenson found no significant relationship, positive or negative, between orientations toward separation of church and state and civil religious belief. Wimberley and Christenson (1980:39) conclude that civil religious issues are separate from issues of church-state separation because American society has no observable organizational structure devoted exclusively to civil religion. This conclusion would support the hypothesis that American civil religion is in the process of differentiating from denominationalism and politics.

Summary

The major point of consensus found in all of the theories and empirical studies cited in this section can be summarized in the form of a proposition.

Proposition I: American civil religion is structurally differentiated from both American religious denominations and American political institutions.

Proposition I is adapted from the structural differentiation hypothesis of John A. Coleman (1970:74) which states that although historically, civil religion has not usually been clearly differentiated from religious and political institutions, in a society such as the United States where religious and political institutions are themselves differentiated, a further differentiation of civil religious belief would be expected. Proposition I is advanced as a device to summarize the sociological literature on American civil religion and differentiaton, and as a point of orientation to guide continued sociological inquiry.

B. The Functions of American Civil Religion

As was previously noted, Phillip Hammond's (1976) bibliographic essay on American civil religion highlights a series of five questions which he sees as central to the study of American civil religion. The first three questions concern the definition of American civil religion, the course of civil religion through American history, and the relationship between American Civil religion and the denominations, and have been addressed in the preceding section. Here, we consider a fourth question asked by Hammond (1976:171), "*Why* would this nation or any nation develop a civil religion?" Hammond's question can be answered by posing a corollary question — what *functions* does civil religion perform for society? The search for an adequate answer begins with an examination of the traditional functions of religion in society. It should be determined whether or not American civil religion performs a specialized version of traditional religious functions pertaining to the citizen's and the society's role concerning issues of ultimate reality. Many of the theoretical and empirical studies already discussed have been concerned with the functions of civil religion. Pertinent studies are re-assessed here if they contain information relevant to particular civil religious functions. Some studies are mentioned at several different junctures in the course of the total discussion. The purpose is to focus upon the *issue* of the functions of civil religion, rather than to pursue any one study in depth. The discussion concludes with the formulation of a theoretical proposition concerning the functions of civil religion in American society.

In order to determine if American civil religion performs a specialized version of the functions performed by other religious symbol systems, it is necessary to determine and clarify the function of religion for society. Although the functions of religion have been conceived of and expressed by sociologists of religion in various terms, three functions would most likely be acknowledged by most social scientists as important indicators of religion's force in society, (1) the integrative role of religion, (2) the legitimating role of religion, and (3) the prophetic role of religion. These three functions of religion partially overlap with one another in everyday life, but can be analyzed separately. The functions of religion for the individual, such as providing values for identity formation and personal meaning creation are acknowledged, but will not be explored in detail here.

1. Religion as a Source of Integration

The observation that religion may act as a source of integration stems from the Durkheimian tradition. Durkeim (1912/1926:47) defined religion according to this function as a system of sacred beliefs and practices uniting believers into a moral community. Durkheim identified the integrating function of religion in a primitive, undifferentiated society in which members manifested their interdependence through moral bonds, strengthened by religion. Modern societies are structurally differentiated and frequently religiously plural, factors that call into question the integrative power of religion. Phillip Hammond (1974) argues that Durkheim fails to go beyond the primitive stage of mechanical solidarity to account for modern religious forms such as pluralism. Hammond agrees with Durkheim that in undifferentiated societies with mechanical solidarity integration is expressed in religious sentiments. But Hammond concludes that the integrating function of religion is an inadequate explanation of the organic solidarity chacacteristic of religiously plural societies such as the United States. Hammond would reword Durkheim's thesis to state that rather than religion producing the cohesive society, cohesion is perceived to have a religious quality. Because conflict threatens societal cohesion, institutions that resolve conflict in moden societies will also take on religious qualities. In religiously plural societies, the function of conflict resolution moves away from the domain of the churches and comes under the control of legal institutions. (Hammond, 1974:129).

2. American Civil Religion and Integration

Determining the integrative potential of religion or its functional alternatives in a differentiated society is an important task for the sociologist of religion. If the integratng function of religion cannot be demonstrated in a differentiated society, sociologists like Richard Fenn (1976) reasonably can argue that no overarching religious traditions can unite members and institutions. If, as Hammond suggests, religious functions and meanings shift to differentiating institutions such as the legal system, the possibility of new sources of integration remains open. American civil religion could be a modern, differentiated religious dimension potentially capable of contributing to social integration at times of societal strain or conflict.

a. John A. Coleman

Coleman's (1970) elaboration of Bellah's model of transcendent universal American civil religion assumes that civil religion performs an integrating function by definition, based on Durkheim's classic definition of religion. In Coleman's view, where civil religion is sufficiently differentiated, it may displace organized religion as a primary institutional source of societal cohesion (Coleman, 1970:76). Thus, for Coleman the empirical question becomes one of determining whether or not denominational religion still provides any integration for modern society. Coleman is the only American theorist taking such an extreme position on the integrative function of American civil religion. More typical are the moderate positions of N. J. Demerath II and Phillip Hammond (1967) and Robert Bellah (1975), who propose that American civil religion has integrative potential, but evidence of the actual performance of integration must be left empirically open.

b. N. J. Demerath and Phillip Hammond

Demerath and Hammond (1967:202-204) claim that determining the role of religion for social integration is complicated by the tendency of Americans to assume that "religion" and "denominational religion" are synonymous. When the institution of religion is equated with the denomination, sociologists such as Richard Fenn (1972) may question whether the diversity of denominations can function to integrate a plural society. An alternative conclusion is suggested by Demerath and Hammond (1967:205), who suggest that modern society may have "alternative structural arrangements" for performing integration. They propose that civil religion is one such structural alternative for integrating American society. They attribute the development of civil religion in modern societies primarily to differentiation and pluralism. In a religiously plural society, cognitive religious sentiments become structured apart from ethical religious sentiments. The former become institutionalized in religious organizations, while the latter become institutionalized as the religious dimension of the polity (Demerath and Hammond, 1967:210). Demerath and Hammond believe that a differentiated American civil religion now performs the function of integration for the modern United States. The integrative function of American civil religion is attributed, in part, to the inability of religious organizations to agree theologically and thus provide sufficient unity in the midst of denominational and theological diversity (Demerath and Hammond, 1967:212).

c. Richard Fenn

The position of Richard Fenn on the integrative functions of American civil religion has been discussed in the preceding section in the analysis of Fenn's typology of American civil religion. Fenn views modern society as structurally differentiated beyond the capacities of religious systems to offer any overarching normative basis of integration. At the societal level, American conflicts typically are solved according to pragmatic criteria, not by moral directives (Fenn, 1970:136). Fenn believes that moral choices exist for the individual in modern society, but that there is no overarching normative system which integrates individuals into a similar pattern of meaning and ultimate ends. Fenn would agree with Demerath and Hammond that traditional religious symbol systems no longer serve as primary sources of integration for modern society, but disagrees that civil religion is capable of assuming the function of integration.

d. Conrad Cherry

Cherry (1970), in his symbolic study of American cults of the dead, concludes that American civil religion performs both integrative and divisive functions for American society. In early America, the funeral services of Thomas Jefferson and John Adams performed integrative functions for the new nation, but the funeral services of Robert Kenendy in 1968 were both unifying and divisive for the society. Due to America's class, regional, and racial diversity, different groups react differently to the symbols of American civil religion. Cherry notes that some groups saw Kennedy's death as evidence that national values had failed to unite all citizens. Cherry (1971:19) raises an important issue when he asks how inclusive American civil religion can be in a pluralistic society. For example, can American civil religion include atheism and integrate atheistic citizens? How can American civil religion support the democratic principle opposed to the exclusion of any group and still maintain transcendent ideals? Can the values of American civil religion, which originated in Protestant civic piety, truly integrate America's racial and religious minorities? Can these same values, developed within a particular national tradition, have international integrative potential as Bellah (1967) maintains (Cherry, 1971:19-20)? Despite these questions and the divisions they may represent, Cherry would not agree with Fenn that American civil religion entirely fails to integrate American society. Although modern American society is differentiated along regional, ethnic, and socioeconomic lines, American civil religion constitutes a "national point of view" which may be both integrative and divisive (Cherry, 1970:310). Cherry's analysis is useful in pointing out the sources of divisiveness in American society, but fails to suggest the conditions under which American civil religion may be expected to either integrate or divide.

e. Robert Bellah

Bellah (1975:27) has selected the biblical image of "covenant" to symbolize the integrative function of American civil religion. As we've already noted, the American covenant refers to a normative symbol system, separate from the actual social behavior of Americans. Bellah does not maintain that the potential for unity found in the American covenant has always been fulfulled. Instead, the history of America is a history of the "broken covenant." The image of a broken covenant is itself suggestive of a dialectic. When Bellah (1975:142) states that "today the American civil religion is an empty and broken shell," he does not mean that American civil religion has disappeared from American culture. Instead, the broken covenant signifies a society temporarily unable to be informed by its values, and temporarily unable to institutionalize these values in a binding way.

Bellah would agree with Cherry that American civil religion has the potential for both integration and division. But unlike Cherry, Bellah has a partial explanation for the societal divisions that exist despite the institutionalization of American civil religion. Bellah sees divisions occurring along ideological lines when the transcendent universal values of American civil religion are interpreted by various segments of society in terms of their own theologies or ideologies. For example, there are "the theology of cultural sophisticates and the theology of Bible-believing Christians" (Bellah, 1976a:155). Protestants, Catholics, and Jews may also vary in their interpretations of American civil religion. Varying ideologies, such as those of different political parties, may also emerge. Bellah notes that in some societies the competition among theology, ideology, and civil religion may result in deep societal division. In the United States such extreme divisions largely have been avoided (with the exception of the Civil War) because, despite the fact that American civil religion has not had universal support, neither has it been challenged by any highly popular competing ideology (Bellah, 1976a:155). American civil religion is not integrative by definition. *American civil religion can foster integration only under the conditions of limited competition from alternative theological and ideological systems.*

Unlike Coleman, who assumes that American civil religion integrates society, and unlike Fenn, who assumes that it does not, Bellah allows the question of American civil religion and integration to remain empirically open. As an ideal symbol system, the transcendent, universal, American civil religion offers a moral basis of integration. Under actual historical and social conditions, American civil religion may either succeed or fail as a source of social unity. But, as long as the possibility of integration based on American civil religion exists, Bellah's view of American society must differ drastically from that of Fenn. Commenting on Fenn's description of the collapse of the American moral order, Bellah (1976a:157) observes that Fenn's argument implies that an entirely new system of social relations has emerged in the United States. Bellah calls upon Fenn to provide empirical evidence for his position. If, as Fenn maintains, American society lacks sources of moral integration, it is up to Fenn to document this change and demonstrate how a society so divided can still stand.

3. Religion as a Source of Legitimation

One way religion serves to integrate society is through the legitimation of a moral order. Peter Berger (1967:29) defines legitimation as "socially objectified knowedge that serves to explain and justify the social order." If members of a society do not share common definitions of reality, integration becomes problematic. Because societies attempt to legitimize their institutional arrangements in terms of an ultimate set of values, legitimation falls within the realm of religion. Religion serves as a legitimating agent in social life by providing an ultimate system of meaning for social behavior. Berger (1967:32) observes that while religion is not the only institutional source of legitimation, historically, religion has played an extensive and effective role in "world-maintenance."

In primitive and archaic societies, in which there is no differentiation between religious and political institutions, the political order is typically viewed as a manifestation of the sacred realm. Those in political power are conceived of as gods, or as representatives of a supreme power. Berger (1967:34) calls this the "microcosm/macrocosm scheme of legitimation" because the primitive or archaic society tends to view itself as a microcosm of the larger cosmic order. In modern societies the microcosm/macrocosm relationship tends to break down with the advent of increased societal complexity. Separation of church and state may result in the competition of religious and political systems or legitimation. Complex systems of legitimation tend to emerge in situations where interpretations of reality are being challenged by alternatives. Modern American society is characterized by the differentiation of religious and political institutions and by religious pluralism. Religious pluralism in particular creates a situation in which religious systems of legitimation are in competition with one another. Modern society, faced with the erosion of traditional meaning systems due to pluralism and the resultant competition, has an increased need for legitimating systems. Whether or not civil religion can provide the solution to modern society's need for legitimation is the subject of debate among sociologists of civil religion.

4. American Civil Religion and Legitimation

a. Robert Bellah

The major participants in the debate over the legitimating potential of American civil religion are Robert Bellah, Richard Fenn, and Robert Stauffer. Bellah's Durkheimian model of American civil religion is based on the assumption that social cohesion rests upon common moral and religious meaning systems providing an explanation and justification of the universe (Bellah, 1975:ix). Bellah (1975:x) believes that American civil religion performed the function of legitimation for early American society, and carries the potential for renewal of this function in contemporary times. He admits that the legitimating power of these American values has eroded. The concept of "virtue," for example, has a different meaning for the twentieth century American than for the eighteenth century Puritan (Bellah, 1975:x). Yet, alongside moral erosion has come renewal. Contemporary Americans retain the value of individual freedom, and the concepts of liberty and justice inform the society's treatment of minorities and women to a greater extent today than in earlier times. In Bellah's view, the myths and symbols of American civil religion retain the power to help Americans interpret and legitimate their social experience in the light of transcendent reality (Bellah, 1975:3).

b. Richard Fenn

Richard Fenn, who argues that American society lacks moral integration, additionally assumes that no religiously-based societal source of legitimation exists. In Fenn's view, modern religion provides little beyond a set of personalized meaning structures without societal functions. Personal civil religion may provide meaning for individual identity development, but societal civil religion, which could provide a system of cultural legitimation, is no longer operative in contemporary American life. Instead, American institutions are guided by criteria of functional rationality, having no religious basis (Fenn, 1972:18).

c. Robert Stauffer

Robert Stauffer (1973) critiques the privatistic "end of ideology" view of Fenn. Stauffer suggests that even a technically efficient, means-oriented society requires the operation of some underlying cultural interpretation of the form by which means are accomplished. In Stauffer's view, Fenn has overlooked the fact that a technocratic political system requires its own legitimating worldview, and that functional rationality itself is a legitimating system of meaning. In addition, Stauffer believes that privatists such as Fenn overlook the possibility that social strains may create a demand for new forms of legitimation. Stauffer sees differentiation and the resultant ideological debates in modern society to be fertile ground for the emergence of new ideological systems of legitimation. Stauffer would not argue with Fenn about the importance of the private sphere of religion. Stauffer (1973:423) would retain, however, the recognition that "both persistent and new forms of overarching cultural legitimations. . .do exist." Stauffer would include American civil religion among the potentially enduring forms of overarching cultural legitimation. Although he questions the prophetic function attributed to American civil religion by Bellah, he finds Bellah's work to be a useful model for the identification of modern legitimating systems which emerge in response to national strains.

5. Religion as a Source of Prophecy

The study of religion's prophetic role originated in the Weberian tradition, which distinguished between the priestly and prophetic styles of religious leadership. As Weber (1922) notes, this distinction extends beyond religious leadership into the whole symbol system of religion. Bellah (1975:ix-xi) writes of the prophetic role of religious values which judge and criticize a society that strays too far from them. Demerath and Hammond (1967:212) subdivide religious prophecy into several dimensions. Prophetic influence may be direct or indirect, innovative or supportive of the *status quo*. In addition, it is useful to distinguish between prophetic attempts and successes. The prophetic function of religion must be studied with regard to the conditions facilitating or resisting prophecy, and variations in prophetic impact, such as the amount and direction of change (Demerath and Hammond, 1967:223).

The prophetic role is linked to religion's integrative and legitimating roles. A direct and positive relationship among the three functions could be logically proposed. The greater extent to which a society is legitimized and integrated by a common set of moral understandings, the greater would be the prophetic potential of these same moral values. Those values having the power to inform and unite would also have the power to judge deviation and demand behavior in conformity to higher standards. Bellah (1975:ix) assumes there is a positive relationship between religious legitimation, integration, and prophecy. However, Demerath and Hammond (1967:230) assume an inverse relationship between integration and prophecy, at least within the context of a particular religious organization. It is assumed that the more tightly moral values bind a social group, the less likely the *status quo* will be challenged, as such a challenge would threaten to destroy the very order on which the group is based. It is not the purpose of this analysis to fully answer these questions concerning the conditions leading to religious prophecy and the relationship between prophecy and integration. Rather, the objective is to suggest that these same issues relevant to the sociology of religion are also crucial to the study of the prophetic role of American civil religion.

6. American Civil Religion and Prophecy

A discussion of the prophetic role of American civil religion has already been provided here in chapters two and three, which contrast the integrative, legitimating, folk religion model to the prophetic transcendent universal model of American civil religion. Church historian Sidney Mead was one of the first to elaborate the prophetic potential of American civil religion. In "The Nation with the Soul of a Church" (1967), Mead argues that due to the religiously pluralistic origins of the United States, Americans began looking to the society itself to perform the traditional religious functions of cohesion, personal meaning, and prophecy. Differentiation between religious and political institutions, and religious pluralism are the key processes Mead credits with producing a highly generalized, yet prophetic, American civil religion. The latter is partially separate from the denominations, but stands over them to guard against self-transcendent and particularistic tendencies.

a. Robert Bellah

The sociological model of Robert Bellah has also stressed the prophetic function of American civil religion. He believes that American civil religion is founded on the belief that "the nation is not an ultimate end in itself but stands under transcendent judgement" (Bellah, 1974a:254). American civil religion originated with the belief in a power higher than man and the society, and that belief has been periodically renewed at critical moments in American history. Bellah (1976b:67) interprets the Declaration of Independence as giving clear priority to the individual's relationship with God over his relationship to the state, as exemplified by the upholding of the right of citizens to form a new government if the state should become destructive of individual rights. Additionally he affirms that civil religion has the potential to challenge the authority of American institutions (Bellah, 1967b:167). He cites Lincoln's opposition to the Mexican American War (Bellah, 1967:17) and Lincoln's 1857 speech decrying the Dred Scott decision (Bellah, 1976b:168) as examples of the institutionally critical potential of American civil religion.

Bellah is aware that the transcendent dimension of American civil religion is not always recognized by American society. At times the symbols of American civil religion are used to support a pattern-maintaining public theology, or are twisted into religious nationalism. Religious nationalism emerges when a society fails to remain informed by civil religion's prophetic message. Religious nationalism is a transcendent civil religion turned idolatrous. In Bellah's view, the transcendent and idolatrous applications of American civil religion are not separate forms of civil faith, but are good and evil sides of the same phenomenon. The variables Bellah highlights as intervening in American society to foster the ideology of religious nationalism include the rise of science, the market economy, and industrial capitalism, all of which work together to facilitate nationally self-transcendent interpretations of civil religion (Bellah, 1975:xii).

Bellah's symbol of the broken covenant illustrates that an overarching, meaning-endowing, prophetic American civil religion can be forgotten by a society and its leaders, leaving a nation floundering in internal division, meaninglessness, and national self-transcendence. Each of Bellah's major writings on

American civil religion has stressed the need for the renewal and reinstitutionalization of the original transcendent values of American civil religion. "Civil Religion in America" (1967) concludes with a prophetic call for the application of the underlying ethical principles of American civil religion to current national problems. In *The Broken Covenant* (1975:151) Bellah continues the prophetic warning. Bellah believes that the religious renewal of the transcendent values of American civil religion is essential for the future of American society. However, Bellah is not optimistic about American civil religions' restoration. Despite his own faith, Bellah continues to document the crisis in American civil religion.

b. Richard Fenn

The privatist position on American civil religion, exemplified by Fenn, assumes that the symbols of American civil religion have no overall cultural significance, and therefore, cannot direct prophetic guidance for social change. In particular, he argues that when the symbols associated with American civil religion are used to legitimate existing institutions, their prophetic potential is nullified. Fenn (1976) selects the American mythic theme of building a new Israel as an illustration. Historically, the symbol of Israel was used paradoxically both to strengthen denominational authority when Christians were in the minority, and to facilitate religious pluralism in nations like the United States. Today, the prophetic imagery of the new Israel symbolism is increasingly weakened by differentiation between social and personality systems (Fenn, 1976:161).

Bellah's response to Fenn is a reiteration of the distinction between public theology and transcendent American civil religion. In 1776, the symbolism of an American Israel was a part of public theology, not of transcendent universal civil religion. If the new Israel symbolism was used to reinforce institutional authority, it was only serving the traditional legitimating function of public theology. While, as Bellah notes, American civil religion serves a legitimating function, this legitimation is always conditional. Bellah (1976b:167) recalls Weber's perspective on religious legitimation, which holds that "legitimation always involves an element of contingency, a linking of two spheres, the political order and ultimate reality, that are not in principle fused." A civil religion conditionally legitimates American culture, but because it is not fused with the culture, it is free to offer prophetic judgement when the nation violates its own transcendent ideals.

c. Martin Marty

In *The New Shape of American Religion* (1959) Marty describes an American folk religion lacking the moral and theological substance of denominational religion. American civil religion, in order to be acceptable to Americans of divergent religious backgrounds, is necessarily overgeneralized to the point of losing moral content and prophetic vigor. Americans might still believe in God, but the God of American civil religion has become "an American jolly good fellow" (Marty, 1959:39) unlikely to be the source of prophetic judgement. In a more recent adaptation of his original work, Marty (1974) expands his treatment of American civil religion to include four sub-types of civil religion. Marty delineates two basic types of civil religion, one divinely transcendent and the other nationally self-transcendent. The former, transcendent civil religion, places God above the nation, while the latter, self-transcendent civil religion, stresses national self-worship. Within each basic type of civil religion there are two styles of religious leadership. Civil religion may be either celebrative, affirmative, culture building, and therefore priestly, or challenging and judgemental, and therefore prophetic (Marty, 1974:144-145). Figure 6 summarizes Marty's typology.

Figure 6
Types of American Civil Religion (Marty, 1974)

Central Theological Affirmation

	Divine Transcendence	*National Self-Transcendence*
Religious Style		
Priestly	Priest: Eisenhower	Priest: Nixon
Prophetic	Prophet: Lincoln	Prophet: Sidney Mead

Priestly transcendent civil religion is the version of folk religion that received ritual expression through Dwight D. Eisenhower's personal style of fostering national cohesion during the cold war years. The latter combined divine transcendence and integrative affirmative qualities. (Marty, 1974:146-147). Prophetic transcendent civil religion is illustrated by Abraham Lincoln's prophetic role during the Civil War, in which he called upon both sides of the conflict to seek knowledge of and obedience to God's will. Priestly self-transcendent civil religion most closely approximates religious nationalism. The nation replaces God as ultimate authority. An extreme example of priestly self-transcendent religion is the John Birch Society's patriotic version of America. The final type, prophetic self-transcendent civil religion, refers to universalistic civil religion derived from humanistic American ideals. Marty (1974:1953-154) sees Sidney Mead (1967) as a contemporary prophet of self-transcendent civil religion who tends to ignore God in his advocacy of a world civil religion. Marty's evaluation of Mead is debatable (see Richey and Jones, 1974:15-16) and unless a stronger case can be built, prophetic self-transcendent civil religion is the weakest cell in Marty's typology. Despite the limitations of the typology, it is useful for suggesting variations in the theological orientations of civil religion, and the possibility of a dynamic tension between the priestly and prophetic modes of civil religious expression.

d. Empirical Studies

1. Thomas and Flippen: There has been little direct empirical study of the prophetic function of American civil religion, but a few studies of the transcendent dimension of civil religion provide relevant data. Thomas and Flippen's (1972) content analysis of the editorials of a national sample of newspapers published during the Honor America Weekend, July 4, 1970, was designed as a test of the transcendent dimension of American civil religion. The coding instrument, intended to distinguish between transcendent civil religion items and their nontranscendent equivalents, relied on the mention of God as the main criterion of transcendent civil religiosity. Analysis of data revealed that while a fairly large number of *non*transcendent civil themes were expressed in the Honor America editorials, few of the themes specifically referred to God.

Evaluation of the measurement instrument used by Thomas and Flippen suggests an alternative interpretation of their findings. They required that reference to a transcendent being be explicit, while *implied* transcendence was coded as nontranscendent. For example, "God has blessed America" would be coded as a civil religion item while "America has been blessed" would be coded as a secular item (Thomas and Flippen, 1972:221). Many sociologists of religion would not agree that belief in a supreme being should be the defining criterion of religiosity. Presence or absence of a sense of ultimate reality is a commonly accepted contemporary criterion of religiosity (e.g., Bellah, 1964; Yinger, 1963; Stauffer, 1973), even though this criterion is difficult to operationalize. Thomas and Flippen's reliance on the mention of God to separate civil religion items from secular items may have unfairly limited the number of items that could be considered religious. Even if it were agreed that a test of Bellah's particular model of transcendent universal American civil religion would require some notion of a transcendent being, it is not evident that the reference to God must be *explicit.* It is not clear that the editorialist who wrote "America has been blessed" did not assume or wish to imply that it was God who did the blessing. Unfortunately, there is no way to measure items that reflect cultural values which may be so generally associated with supernatural origins that the need to state the origins explicitly may be considered unnecessary. Despite the difficulties in developing an accurate measurement of civil religious symbols, Thomas and Flippen's data actually show that secular civil themes were commonly expressed, but the transcendent nature of these themes could not be demonstrated.

2. Jolicoeur and Knowles: Another content analysis, conducted by Jolicoeur and Knowles (1978), using a different measurement instrument than that used by Thomas and Flippen, reports evidence of transcendent civil religious values among Masonic fraternal orders. Data were collected from 1964 to 1974 issues of *The New Age,* a national Masonic journal. Unlike the editorials reviewed by Thomas and Flippen, nearly half (46.5%) of *The New Age* issues mentioned "God." Belief in God was frequently cited in the context of references to the United States, American history, and national goals. In the Masonic Journal, the source of American strength and prosperity are attributed to belief in a supreme being (Jolicoeur and Knowles, 1978:12). Jolicoeur and Knowles found transcendent civil religious beliefs expressed in a traditional conservative journal, while Thomas and Flippen reported the absence of these beliefs in a more heterogeneous sample of newspapers. Unfortunately, due to the differences and contradictions between the two measurement instruments, it is not possible to compare the conclusions of the two content analyses in any meaningful way.

3. Ronald C. Wimberley: The most extensive effort to obtain an empirical measurement of transcendent civil religious beliefs is found in the work of Ronald Wimberley and his colleagues. In one of their earliest studies of individual civil religious belief, (Wimberley et al., 1976) items were designed to measure the transcendent aspects of American civil religion discussed by Bellah (1967). The majority of civil religion items mentioned a transcendent God, as in the item, "We should respect the president's authority since his authority is from God." The few items not mentioning a supreme being linked Christianity to the political system, as in "Good Christians aren't necessarily good patriots" (Wimberley et al., 1976:893). Due to the transcendent references in the civil religion indicators, Wimberley (1976:394) is convinced that he has made a valid measurement of the transcendent civil religion of Bellah's model, and not of public theology. Bellah might disagree. Commenting on a paper presented by Wimberley (later published as Wimberley, 1980), Bellah (1976a:155) suggests that Wimberley's measurement instrument measures "a rather conservative brand of public theology" rather than transcendent American civil religion. In response to Bellah, Wimberley (1979) published a replication survey which used some of the original civil religion measurement items, and two new items specifically framed to tap civil religious beliefs derived from American historical documents. Bellah's (1967) analysis had referred to national documents as a major source of transcendent civil religious symbolism. For example, one of Wimberley's new items, "In this country, people have equal, Divinely given rights to life, freedom and the search for happiness" (Wimberley, 1979:60) is derived from the Declaration of Independence. Factor analysis of the replication survey found all of the civil religion items loaded with each other within one factor. Wimberley (1979:61-62) concludes that both the original and new items measured one civil religion dimension representing the transcendent values in Bellah's model. Because Wimberley's research has contributed to the controversy surrounding the measurement of the transcendent aspect of American civil religion, two sets of civil religion items used by Wimberley and his colleagues (Wimberley 1976; 1979) are reproduced in the appendix.

The data concerning the transcendent dimension of American civil religion and its prophetic functions are inconclusive at this stage in the research process. The acknowedgement of a transcendent authority is a necessary, but not sufficient condition for prophecy. The findings of Jolicoeur and Knowles, who encounter a high proportion of transcendent civil religious statements in a national journal published by a traditional fraternal order, and those of Christenson and Wimberley (1978) who found a positive association between transcendent civil religious beliefs and religious and political conservatism could be interpreted as support for the Demerath and Hammond's (1967) hypothesis that there is an inverse relationship between religious integration and prophecy. Additional empirical study is required before sociologists can confirm or disconfirm Bellah's thesis of American civil religion's prophetic role.

4. *Sites and Mueller:* The most direct empirical test of the prophetic dimension of American civil religion is found in Sites and Mueller's (1978) analysis of sermons delivered on the occasion of the American Bicentennial, July 4, 1976. In a simple random sample of sermons delivered in sixty Protestant and Catholic churches, the majority of sermons contained both priestly and prophetic civil religious themes. Prophetic themes were those components of the sermons citing threats to the American heritage and social problems that could be solved only with God's help. Government scandal and corruption were the most frequently cited threats to America, followed by poverty, racism, prejudice, big business and the concentration of wealth, and military involvement and the

misuse of power. The majority of prophetic themes found in the sermons coincided with the issues Bellah (1975) mentions as examples of the broken covenant between the American nation and its transcendent authority. Sites and Mueller report some denominational variation with respect to prophetic Bicentennial themes. For example, one-half of the Catholic clergy and one-third of the Episcopal clergy *failed to mention any prophetic issues.* It is possible that a denomination's tendency to take a prophetic civil religious stance is linked to the denomination's historical inclination toward either a priestly or a prophetic orientation. Nevertheless, some clergy in every denomination sampled mentioned prophetic themes. Sites and Mueller conclude that the prophetic force in American civil religion is alive and can be evidence in the sermons of contemporary American clergy.

e. Conclusion

There has been considerable theoretical argument, accompanied by scant empirical research, concerning the functions of American civil religion in contemporary American society. The extremes in the debate are represented by Bellah's model, which argues that American civil religion can perform the specialized religious functions of integration, legitimation, and prophecy for American society; and by Fenn's privatist position, which maintains that American civil religion is incapable of performing any societal function in contemporary times. There is,however, one common point of agreement among the participants in the debate. All agree that traditional religious symbol systems have become so differentiated and privatized in American society as to be weakened in their contributions to American integration, legitimation, and prophetic judgement. Fenn additionally assumes that civil religion has become completely privatized along with denominational religion. Fenn does not specify what social institutions, if any, do perform the functions associated with social integration and legitimation. If religion and civil religion no longer provide the bonds and sources of guidance for American society, the question of societal self-maintenance becomes problematic. As Stauffer suggests, even a technological, rational society requires some underlying cultural interpretation of the form by which means are accomplished and requires some agreement on this interpretation to remain even minimally integrated. American civil religion is a potential contributer to such legitimation and integration for contemporary society. It remains for empirical studies to test this ostensibly logical, although still unconfirmed, hypothesis.

A test of the prophetic function of American civil religion is more problematic. Stauffer (1973:424) sees American civil religion as an institutional alternative potentially able to assume the integrative and legitimating functions traditionally performed by religion in society. However, Stauffer is skeptical of the prophetic function which Bellah attributes to American civil religion. There has not yet been sufficient empirical study of the prophetic dimension of American civil religion to substantially support either Stauffer's or Bellah's position. Future research into the prophetic function would best view prophecy as did Weber, as one dimension of a continuum composed of priestly and prophetic styles. Elaboration of the conditions under which a religion is more likely to manifest institutional reinforcement or challenge would be helpful in determining if American civil religion has primarily reflected priestly or prophetic orientations.

While it has not yet been demonstrated that American civil religion performs specialized religious functions, this hypothesis is promising. The hypothesis can be stated in the form of a proposition designed to follow Proposition I which proposed that American civil religion is structurally differentiated from its closest institutional neighbors, religious denominations and political institutions. The structural differentiation hypothesis of Proposition I is logically accompanied by the hypothesis of functional differentiation stated in Proposition II.

Proposition II: American civil religion performs specialized religious functions performed neither by the denominations nor by political institutions.

Both Propositions I and II are adapted from John A. Coleman's (1970:76) evolutionary theory of civil religion. Proposition II is concerned only with the performance, by civil religion, of traditional religious functions performed within the distinct province of civil religion's influence, which concerns the roles of the citizen and the society in relation to conditions of ultimate meaning. Even those who would disagree with Proposition II concur that in a society characterized by religious and political differentiation, neither religious or political institutions exclusively perform the functions of integration, legitimation, and prophetic guidance. The institutional field is thus opened for other symbol systems, such as civil religion, to perform specialized contemporary version of the traditional functions of religion.

C. American Civil Religion and Other Institutions

The two preceding sections of this chapter have considered a series of questions posed by Phillip Hammond as central to the study of American civil religion. In this section we turn to Hammond's (1976:171) final question, "What *institutions* promulgate, transmit, maintain, and modify American civil religion?" Thus far we have presented arguments and evidence suggesting that while the values of American civil religion are congruent with the values of American religious and political institutions, American civil religion remains structurally and functionally differentiated from these institutions. Contemporary American civil religion appears to be controlled neither by the religious denominations nor the political system, although civil religious values are manifest in both institutions at a high level of generality. The relationship between American civil religion and other American institutions may be exptected to follow a similar pattern. The major institutions to which scholars of American civil religion have addressed themselves are public educational institutions, religio-civic voluntary associations, and economic institutions.

1. American Public Education

In *Piety in the Public Schools* (1970), Robert Michaelson presents an historical analysis of the relationships among the American public schools, American denominations, and American civil religion. According to Michaelson, there was an early, close relationship between American religious and educational institutions. The values of evangelical religion were formative elements in the rise of formal education in colonial America. Institutions of higher education, such as Harvard and Princeton, were founded to serve the primary function of Protestant ministerial education. The establishment of the common school was itself a major cause of educated clergy, many of whom dedicated themselves to developing a nationwide system of general education. On his visit to the United States in the 1830's Alexis de Tocqueville observed that American education was largely "entrusted to the clergy" (quoted in Michaelson, 1970:51). Although Tocqueville's statement is an exaggeration, early American educational systems, including the public schools, were influenced by traditional religious values and were expected to produce pious and moral citizens. American schools have also traditionally served the civil religious function of social integration. Michaelson (1970:57) observes that the school's religious functions extended beyond the provision of moral education to encourage the development of a common American identity. In the late nineteenth and early twentieth centuries, a series of legal decisions both precipitated and reflected an increasing differentiation between public education and American religious organizations. Today, public education no longer manifests particularistic religious teachings, and public schools are neither expected nor allowed to perform the function of religious education. Although the special religious functions of the public schools have declined due to differentiation of educational and religious institutions, public schools continue to perform a civil religious function for American society. By use of historical data, this process of differentiation and its effects on the religious and civil religious functions of public education can be documented.

a. *Religious and Civil Religious Functions of Early American Public Education*

Bernard Bailyn (1960:21) has observed that, during the early colonial period, the major institutions of socialization and acculturation were the family, community, and church, rather than the school. It was not until the end of the colonial period that formal schooling became more universal, and thus a significant source of socialization. The Great Awakenings stimulated the founding of a number of colonial colleges, whose graduates in turn established institutions and standards for all levels of education. The awakeners attempted to build an educational system that fostered religious piety as well as knowledge. Michaelson credits evangelical religion as the major influence on early American formal education, but notes that evangelically influenced schools were often directed toward patriotism as well as religion. The expectations of higher education were extended to all educational levels. To the extent that American schools typically performed religious and civil functions along with general educational functions, these several tasks of the school were not always in harmony, and conflict between religious particularists and generalists was typical. Particularists were motivated to institutionalize denominational and/or sectarian religious values even in the public schools, while generalists advocated nondenominational, nonsectarian approaches to morality in public education. Archbishop Hughes of New York exemplified the particularist viewpoint. He conceived of religion in a denominationally-influenced public educational system. Horace Mann and John Dewey represented the generalist viewpoint. Both were influenced by the deistic, Jeffersonian philosophy of education which stressed the morality of natural, nondenominational religion. Mann opposed sectarianism and, along with Dewey, advocated that the public schools be based on a "common faith" in humanistic, democratic values.

Figure 7
Significant Court Cases Related to Religion and the Public School*

Short Designation	Name of Case	Date	Central Issue	Disposition
Pierce	Pierce v. Society of Sisters 268 U. S. 510	1925	Oregon's mandatory public school attendance statute.	Unconstitutional (unanimous)
Cochran	Cochran v. Lousiana 281 U.S. 370	1930	Statute providing use of tax money for books for children attending public and other schools.	Upheld (unanimous)
Everson	Everson v. Board of Education, 330 U.S. 1	1947	Tax subsidy for bus transportation for children attending Catholic schools (N.J.).	Upheld (5-4)
Allen	Board of Education v. Allen 392 U.S. 236	1968	N.Y. statute requiring tax-subsidized textbooks for parochial and private school students.	Upheld (6-3)
Gobitis	Minersville v. Gobitis 310 U.S. 586	1940	Required daily flag salute in public school (Minersville, Pa.).	Upheld (8-1)
Barnette	West Virginia v. Barnette 319 U.S. 624	1943	State Board of Education ruling requiring flag salute in public schools.	Unconstitutional (6-3)
McCollum	McCollum v. Board of Education, 333 U.S. 203	1948	Released-time program on school premises (Champaign, Ill.).	Unconstitutional (8-1)
Zorach	Zorach v. Clauson 343 U.S. 306	1952	Released-time program off school premises (N.Y.C.).	Upheld (6-3)
Engel	Engel v. Vitale 370 U.S. 421	1962	New York State Board of Regents composed and school-sponsored prayer.	Unconstitutional (6-1)
Schempp	School District v. Schempp Murray v. Curlett 874 U.S. 203	1963	School-sponsored prayer (Lord's Prayer) and devotional Bible reading (Pa. and Baltimore).	Unconstitutional (8-1)

*Adapted from Michaelson, 1970; 194.

Early in the conflict between particularists and generalists, both sides prevailed in certain respects. Particularism influenced public education into the twentieth century. Until the United States Supreme Court decisions of the twentieth century weakened religion's influence on the public schools, authorized prayer and Bible reading were commonplace features of the American public school system. Although advocates of these practices viewed them as nonsectarian, they were largely Protestant in orientation, usually based on the King James version of the Bible and utilizing the Protestant version of the Lord's Prayer. However, as particularism slowly receded, the civil religious function of public education emerged more clearly. During the late 1800s and early 1900s, when America experienced its heaviest waves of European immigrants, the public school was seen as *the* major institution for the Americanization and democratization of new citizens. Civics, citizenship, and patriotism courses were infused into the public school curriculum. The public schools became instrumental in performing the civil religious function of social integration for America's immigrant populations.

There is historical evidence that the American public educational system performed both religious and civil religious functions from colonial times into the twentieth century. Often these functions were in competition or conflict. As the twentieth century progressed, the sectarian influence in public schools would gradually decline, leaving civil religion as the only institutionalized form of religious expresson remaining in American public education.

b. Differentiation of Public Education from Religion

The differentiation of American public education from religion is most clearly evidenced by twentieth-century judicial decisions limiting the role of religion in the public schools. Over the past sixty years, the United States Supreme Court has ruled on a number of important cases. Michaelson (1970:194) presents a summary table of significant court cases (see figure 7).

The first significant Supreme Court rulings of the twentieth century concerned the relationship between public schools and private, parochial schools. In 1925, in *Pierce,* the United States Supreme Court unanimously ruled against Oregon's mandatory public school attendance statute, thus supporting the right of children to attend private and religious schools. In the *Cochran, Everson,* and *Allen* decisions, the Court ruled that tax-supported services, such as school books and bus transportation, provided to public school children must be extended to children attending private and religious schools (Michaelson, 1970:193). Although the decision to extend services paid for by the public to students of religious schools might appear to result in the mixing of public and religious domains, these decisions actually aided the survival of separate systems of religious education. By upholding the right to private and religious education, the Court helped insure that religious alternatives to public education would continue to be available.

The dominant direction of United States Supreme Court opinion on religion and public education began to emerge in the 1940s. In 1940, in *Cantwell v. Connecticut,* the provisions of the First Amendment of religion were extended to the states through the Fourteenth Amendment. The court ruled that the states, like the federal government, may not establish a church or enact laws that support any or all religions.

Later the Court applied the logic of *Cantwell* to the *McCollum* decision, striking down a released-time education program on public school grounds in Champaign, Illinois. The program offered religious instruction during school time on school premises. Although the released-time program was voluntary, the plaintiff claimed that her son had been harrassed for non-participation (Michaelson, 1970:196-197). The *McCollum* decision represented a strict separationist position which was characterized by Justice Black as "a wall of separation between Church and State" (quoted in Michaelson, 1970:197). In 1952 separation became accommodation as the Court upheld a released-time religious education program held off school premises (*Zorach*). Although the *Zorach* decision was interpreted by some legal scholars as a softening of the separationist stance of *McCollum* (Michaelson, 1970:198), the decision was still congruent with the concept of differentiation between religious and public education. The Supreme Court at no time acted to destroy the alternative of a separate system of religious education, as long as it was clearly separate, physically and temporally, from public education. The *Engel* and *Schempp* decisions of the 1960s reaffirmed the "wall" between public and religious institutions when public school-sponsored prayer and devotional Bible reading were ruled unconstitutional. Two essential factors in this decision were the "identification of the prayer as religious" and the decision that its use constituted "an establishment of religion" (Michaelson, 1970:194, 207). The Court rulings of the 1960s illustrate the trend toward differentiation.

The immediate impacts of the Supreme Court's separationist decisions on the American denominations were varied. While most Roman Catholic leaders opposed the decisions, Jewish and liberal Protestant groups supported them. A fear of rising secularization characterized the groups in opposition, such as conservative Protestants. Michaelson (1970:232) notes, however, that as time passed many opponents of the separationist decisions changed their attitudes. In 1963, the National Council of Churches of Christ supported the *Engel* decision as offering an opportunity to reexamine the issue of religious values and public education. The United Presbyterian Church in the U.S.A., which in the 1950s had issued a pamphlet identifying "our schools" as "a bulwark for our Protestant concept of morality, democracy and freedom," passed a statement in 1963 supporting *Engel* (quoted in Michaelson, 1970:233). In 1964, The Lutheran Church in America declared that its members should not be alarmed over *Engel* and *Schempp.* American Catholics were much slower to accept separationism, but the positive ecumenical statements on education by Vatican II led to a certain relaxation of Catholic opposition (Michaelson, 1970:234). Michaelson (1970:235) concludes that the separationist decisions of the United States Supreme Court and the differentiation of public education from religion, which resulted from the decisions, ultimately had a dual effect on American religious groups. Initially, the separationist doctrine polarized religious opinion and organizations. But, ultimately the separationist decisions facilitated inter-religious dialogue.

c. Public Education and Americian Civil Religion

The Supreme Court's separationist decisions promoted the institutional differentiation of American public education from religion. The religious content of public education was limited to the "objective study" of religion or to "ceremonies of a civic, patriotic or secular nature" in which religious terms were used (Michaelson, 1970:226). Civic expression remained the only avenue of religious expression officially tolerated in the American public school. In the *Engel* decision, Justice Black pointed out that, although schools cannot sponsor religious exercises, they are free to sponsor patriotic exercises. The fact that American patriotism traditionally possesses a religious dimension complicates the issue of separating religion from public instructional content. Supreme Court decisions on the issue of civil religious expression in public schools have generally maintained that religion can be tolerated in schools if it is contained in a patriotic, rather than a religious, ceremony (Michaelson, 1970:208-209). American public school students may recite the Declaration of Independence and sing the "Star Spangled Banner," both of which contain reference to God. Although the court did not label such rites as civil religion, they contain an acceptable reference to the religious dimension of the polity. The Court sidestepped the issue of the civil religiosity of the pledge of allegiance to the American flag. In *West Virginia v. Barnett* (1943), the Court ruled that the state could not require students to publically profess a "patriotic creed," but the grounds for the decision concerned freedom of *speech* rather than freedom of religion sections of the First Amendment (Michaelson. 1970:210-211). In the arena of public school education, the Court has not ruled, other than in *Barnette,* on the restriction of civil religious expression in schools. Civil religious ceremony is one of the few remaining institutional outlets for religious expression in American public education.

Although the religious content of public education has been severely restricted by the Supreme Court, there has been no effort or intention to limit the *moral* dimension of public education. In 1951, the Educational Policies Commission of the National Educational Association recommended that public schools emphasize values shared by all Americans and become a major institutional source of socialization of these values. Values that the Commission agreed were common to the American people include the ideals of moral equality, brotherhood, respect for human personality, and spiritual enrichment (Michaelson:1970:242). This set of humanistic values, which does not contain reference to a supreme being or to a denominational creed, is representative of American civil religion of either the folk religion or common faith models. Despite the humanistic orientation, the Commission was careful to stress the spiritual nature of these values, perhaps to reassure those who feared complete secularization of the public educational system (Michaelson, 1970:242). The values were also selected to represent ideals Americans have in common, since the public schools have traditionally tried to perform an integrative function for society.

In the past, American public schools democratized and integrated the immigrant. In more recent times, the public school has been the primary American institution charged with the moral task of racial integration (*Brown v. Board of Education*). In contemporary society, as the school continues to assume functions traditionally performed by American families and religious organizations, expectations for schools to serve religious functions are likely to increase, rather than decline. Because the Supreme Court ruled that public schools cannot become an establishment of religion, the religious function of the schools is increasingly expressed in civil religious terms, and focused on civil religious functions. Public schools are expected to socialize students to the civil religious values of equality, brotherhood, and respect for individual personality. These values are general and are intended to overarch the values of particular religious organizations, ethnic and racial groups, and class divisions. Public schools are expected to produce individuals who are socialized to these values, and thus able to participate in an integrated common society. This expectation of social integration has not always been realistic. Whether or not the schools succeed in fostering generalized civil religious values that can truly overarch national divisions is, of course, the basic challenge to American civil religion addressed by Bellah (1975) as the "broken covenant." The American public schools have historically served as a vehicle of the American covenant, and today many Americans continue to look to the schools as an institutional source of societal salvation (Michaelson, 1970:254-255).

2. Voluntary Associations

Warner's (1961) symbolic study of Memorial Day celebrations in an American community suggests that civil religion can be practiced by Americans through voluntary associations such as veteran's organizations and religio-civic community groups. Research by Pamela Jolicoeur and Louis Knowles (1978) demonstrates that fraternal orders still provide an avenue of civil religious expression for many Americans today. Jolicoeur and Knowles note that fraternal orders are likely institutional carriers of American civil religion because orders have traditionally performed both religious and civic functions. Fraternal orders are not "churches"or denominations as such, but they engage in ritual celebrations based on shared myths, and affirm a religiously-based morality. Several studies have noted the religious and moral dimenions of fraternal associations (Gist, 1940); Mackenzie, 1967; Schmidt and Babchuk, 1972). Fraternal orders are also major advocates of patriotism and civic virtue. Orders are therefore among the associations most likely to promulgate the symbols of American civil religion (Jolicoeur and Knowles, 1978:4).

Jolicoeur and Knowles studied the Freemasons, an order founded in England in the eighteenth century and which has served as a model for other American fraternal associations. The estimated national membership of the Freemasons is four million adult males, and it encompasses ten million persons through affiliated organizations for families of members. Data concerning Freemasonry were collected from, 1964 to 1974, issues of *The New Age,* the largest national Masonic journal and the official journal of the Southern Jurisdiction of Scottish Rite Freemasonry, representing Masons in thirty-five states. Sixty percent of the 482 articles sampled were concerned with general topics, and 40 percent with topics specifically related to Masonry. Among the articles devoted to general topics, 31 percent concerned American institutions and the American way of life. 27.2 percent concerned religion or civil religion. The remainder of the articles dealt with historical subjects such as the founding of the nation. God was mentioned in 46.5 percent of all articles in the sample. The Constitution was cited in 19.2 percent, and the founding fathers were referred to in 21.6 percent (Jolicoeur and Knowles, 1978:10-11). Jolicoeur and Knowles interpret these findings as confirming the hypothesis that Freemasonry is devoted to the maintenance of American civil religion.

The Masonic model of American civil religion differs somewhat from the transcendent universal model of Bellah. Both the Masons and Bellah would be categorized in Marty's typology of kinds of civil religion (see figure 6) as representatives of transcendent civil religion, which envisions a transcendent God standing in judgement of society. Although both the Masons and Bellah agree on the divinely transcendent nature of American civil religion, they differ on the content of the prophetic message. According to *The New Age,* "the most serious challenges to the American way of life are Communism, creeping Federal control of the nation, and civil disobedience" (Jolicoeur and Knowles, 1978:17). In contrast, Bellah (1975), cites capitalism, racism, and sexism as major threats to the American covenant. Other differences between these two models are revealed by Jolicoueur and Knowles's data. While Bellah sees Abraham Lincoln as a major prophet of American civil religion, *The New Age* articles contained more references to George Washington (12.7 percent of the sampled articles) than to Lincoln (3.6 percent). The Freemasons emphasize the Revolutionary period and see the Constitution and Bill of Rights as symbols of the personal freedoms guaranteed to Americans by the government. *The New Age* gives little attention to Civil War symbolism and its themes of sacrifice and rebirth which signify to Bellah the dissolution and renewal of the American covenant. The civil religion of the Masons is essentially conservative, emphasizing the defense of American institutions, while Bellah's civil religion challenges existing institutional arrangements to renew the spirit of the covenant.

Jolicoeur and Knowles's findings are congruent with Wimberley's (1976) data which show a positive association between American civil religious beliefs and political conservatism. Jolicoeur and Knowles believe, however, that although the Masons hold a particular interpretation of civil religion, considerable diversity of views exists among other voluntary associations. Jolicoeur and Knowles (1978:18) suggest that Bellah's model of a universal transcendent American civil religion is an ideal type within which there is variation in functional reality. Fraternal orders may function as conservative, civil religious, denomination-like, class-defending voluntary bastions, while other voluntary associations, such as the human potential groups and organizations like Transcendental Meditation, may potentially function as revolutionary civil religious "cults". Bellah (1974b:41) believes that the latter type of associations are "revolutionary" in the sense that they could foster a significant social change based on a movement away from reliance on nationalism and technology. Bellah admits that these groups are not currently capable of organizing revolutionary forms of change at the social and cultural levels. The empirical findings of Jolicoeur and Knowles and Bellah's ideas suggest that future research on voluntary associations as a vehicle for the practice of American civil religion would be fruitful. Research efforts should focus upon voluntary associations fostering the values of American civil religion, classification of the associations' ideologies along a conservatism-utopianism continuum, and exploration of the relationship between these associations and other institutional carriers of American civil religion.

3. The Economy

According to Robert Bellah (1975) the values of American civil religion are in conflict with central values of corporate capitalism. Civil religious and capitalistic values emerged together in the early history of the nation, but have since become

widely divergent. Hiding behind the facade of individualism, corporate development has created a means-oriented economic system uninformed by ultimate
concerns. A break in the American covenant is the result.

a. The History of Utilitarian Individualism

Bellah sees the American nation born under a dual myth. From the bibilical
tradition, Americans conceived of themselves as "God's chosen people" directed
to build a "new Israel" in the new world. The self-transcendent possibilities implied in the concept of a chosen people were tempered by the belief in a transcendent, prophetic God. This relationship between citizen and deity is what Bellah
calls the "American covenant." A second powerful American myth has been
utilitarian individualism. Utilitarian individualism originated in ancient Greek
philosophy and has been carried to the modern era by Thomas Hobbes, John
Locke, and later by the social Darwinists of the late nineteenth century. Utilitarian
individualism has run parallel to biblically-based American myths, both interac-
ting historically in complex "relations of attraction and repulsion" (Bellah,
1974b:34). However, there are also points of conjunction between American civil
religion and utilitarian individualism. Both myths stress individualism, freedom,
and morality, although for different purposes (Bellah, 1974b:34-35). Ultimately,
biblical tradition was coopted by the utilitarians to the extent that religious and
civil religious values were used to legitimate the achievement of self-interest. The
American rights of life, liberty, and the pursuit of happiness were celebrated by
utilitarian individualists as the right to pursue wealth and profit through the
private enterprise system (Bellah, 1975:121).

b. Corporate Capitalism

Although the pure instrumentality of industrial capitalism was originally hid-
den behind the facade of civil religious values, the relationship between American
civil religion and modern capitalism has become increasingly tenuous. Bellah
(1975:130-131) believes that "the system of corporate industry that has grown up in
the last century undermines essential American values and constitutional order."
Far from insuring individual rights and freedoms, corporate growth has dimin-
ished the power of the individual citizen. As examples, Bellah notes the decline of
the small private business and the near disappearance of the autonomous family
farm. Today, the average American is a wage-earner in corporate industry or
agribusiness. Along with the loss of economic autonomy, Bellah believes that individual citizens have lost political power to corporate hands. Today, political
decision making is based on utilitarian considerations of corporate profit, at the
expense of personal piety and/or public virtue. Bellah observes that the supposed
benefits of the American economy, are still not available to certain segments of
the populaton and are ultimately unsatisfying even to many who achieve them
(Bellah, 1975:135). Analyzing the social protest movements of the 1960s and early
1970s, which were notable for their inclusion of middle-class, educated American
youth, Bellah concludes that these protest movements were symptomatic of a national religious crisis. He cites the civil rights movement led by Dr. Martin Luther

King, Jr. as an example of religiously based response to the failures of utilitarian individualism (Bellah 1974b:36). He expresses the hope that some of the anti-utilitarian religious movements of the 1970s will provide visions which could serve as inspiration to renew the American covenant. In the economic sphere, Bellah (1975:136) advocates a form of "decentralized democratic socialism" which, unlike the anti-individualistic socialism of the U.S.S.R., China, and Cuba, would strike a balance between individual and societal needs. He is not naively optmistic about either religious renewal or economic change in the United States. A critical test of the viability of contemporary American civil religion is its very difficult task of informing an economic system with a structure of ultimate meaning.

Bellah's critic, Richard Fenn, essentially agrees with Bellah that the contemporary American economy operates outside the context of ultimacy. Fenn believes that modern economies become functional alternatives to religion and contain the sources of their own legitimacy (Fenn 1972:17). Both Bellah and Fenn agree that the ideology of American corporate capitalism is incongruent with the values of American civil religion. Disagreement between Bellah and Fenn exists only on the level of response to the incongruency and recommendations for the future of the nation. Fenn records and analyzes the differentiation of economic and religious institutions, a process he sees as smooth and evolutionary. Bellah registers concern that economic institutions are increasingly disharmonious with traditional American values, a process he observes as conflictual and precipitous of both reactionary and revolutionary social movements. Bellah is also not unwilling to respond to what he sees as a crisis of meaning with a prophetic call for the establishment of an economic system congruent with the values of American civil religion. Another, perhaps synthetic, position is offered by Robert Stauffer (1973). Stauffer believes that even a utilitarian economy requires some overarching basis of legitimacy. The renewal of American civil religion could provide this legitimacy, or new ideological systems may emerge in the future to provide legitimacy and guidance to the technological economic sector of American society.

c. Conclusion

There is little sociological research on the relationship between American civil religion and other American institutions. While three relevant studies are summarized in this chapter, only one (Jolicoeur and Knowles, 1978) is based on quantititive empirical research methods. Current research, although quite limited, supports the hypothesis that most American institutions are in the process of differentiating from both traditional religion and civil religion. The institutions likely to be least differentiated from American civil religion are the traditional institutions of socialization and integration: the family, religious organizations, religio-civic voluntary associations, and educational institutions. These institutions are exptected to manifest civil religious symbols as a high level of generality. Quantitative research by Jolicoeur and Knowles (1978) and historcal research by Michaelson (1970) support this hyphothesis. Institutions performing instrumental functions, such as the economy and communications media, are expected to exhibit the most differentiation from American civil religion. According to Thomas and Flippen (1972), Fenn (1978), and even Bellah (1975), it is questionable whether civil religious symbols continue to infuse these institutons today. Because available data are so limited, these hypotheses are supported only tentatively. The field is now open for sociologists to respond to Hammond's (1976:171) important question, "What *institutions* promulgate, transmit, maintain, and modify American civil religion?"

CHAPTER 5

CIVIL RELIGION AND RELIGIOUS EVOLUTION

A. Introduction

In the preceding chapter two propositions are stated, proposing that American civil religion is structurally and functionally differentiated from American religious and political institutions. The structural and functional differentiation of these institutions have implications for a theory of civil religious evolution. Coleman (1970) believes that if American civil religion is differentiated from other American institutions, this phenomenon parallels basic evolutionary trends associated with modernization. This chapter explores an evolutionary approach to the study of American civil religion by first examining a number of sociological theories of religious change and evolution. Both classical and contemporary theories are included. Two primary criteria guide the selection of theories for consideration, the strength of the theory's contribution to the sociology of religious change, and the theory's applicability to the study of civil religious evolution. Analysis and comparison of theories leads to the proposal of a third and final proposition concerning American civil religion and cultural evolutionary patterns. Because each of the theories under consideration proposes that in some way religious evolution results in secularization, the use of the term "secularization" will first be addressed.

B. *The Concept of Secularization in Theories of Religious Evolution*

On the most general level of anaysis, each of the selected theories of religious evolution proposes that modernization is associated with secularization. Secularization is a concept that has been used in different ways by different sociologists, resulting in analytic imprecision. Larry Shiner (1968:208-209) notes that, besides the original meaning of secularization (the transfer of lands from church to civil control), there are six other common uses of the term in contemporary sociological research; (1) decline of religion, (2) conformity with "this world," (3) disengagement of society from religion, (4) transposition of religious beliefs and institutions, (5) desacralization of the world, and (6) movement from "sacred" to a "secular" society.

Secularization as "decline of religion " refers to the loss of prestige and social acceptance associated with traditional religion. The decline-of-religion type of secularization is exemplified by the empirical studies reported in a well-known source book in the sociology of religion, Glock and Stark's *Religion and Society in Tension* (1965), which concluded that religion is losing its influence. Secularization viewed as "conformity with 'this world' " would result in a society preoccupied with ordinary activities of daily life maintenance to the extent that religious boundaries between groups would disappear. Typical of this second meaning of secularization is Will Herberg's (1955) thesis that American religious identifications are largely secular in nature and simply reflect acceptable ways of being a good American. Secularization as "disengagement of society from religion" refers to the process by which social institutions separate themselves from religious understanding and control, leaving religion to motivate the private lives of individuals. This is essentially the theory of Peter Berger (1967) and Thomas Luckmann (1967). Shiner criticizes all three definitions of secularization for ambiguity, and points out that they depend upon the definition of religion for derived meaning. For example, it is difficult to show secularization as a decline of religion without specifying some original period of religious domination from which decline could come (Shiner, 1968:210). Shiner (1968:213) suggests that "the more descriptive and neutral" concept of differentiation be substituted for secularization when either "decline of religion" or "disengagement of society from religion" are intended.

The idea of secularization as a "transposition of religious beliefs and institutions" is a fairly precise meaning of secularization, referring to the transformation of sacred phenomena into phenomena controlled by humans. It was through "transposition" that the spirit of capitalism became a secularized version of the Protestant Ethic. "Desacralization of the world" also has a specific meaning based in Weber's process of rationalization and disenchantment. The final definition of secularization, "movement from a 'sacred' to a 'secular' society" is taken from Howard Becker's (1957) analysis. According to Becker, the secular society is the society open to change, not only from religious traditions, but also from any traditional beliefs. Becker's use of secularization is the broadest of the six meanings, as it is derived from a general theory of social change.

Due to the need for conceptual clarification and precise operational definition, Shiner (1968:207) recommends that social scientists either stop using the term secularization, or recognize that it is a general concept covering the three complementary processes of desacralization, differentiation and transposition. Typical of the conceptual imprecision criticized by Shiner is the work of Bryan Wilson, whose conceptualizations of secularization range from disengagement to desacralization to decline of religion. In *Contemporary Transformations of Religion* (1976:16,20,11), for example, Wilson characterizes secularization through the observations that "the presidency that the Church once exercised over social life is gone" (disengagement); "modern society simply denies the authority of the Churches by ignoring them" (decline of religion); and "we can observe a gradual, uneven, at times oscillating trend, towards . . . a 'matter-of-fact' orientation to the world" (desacralization.) Applying Shiner's criteria for clarification, Wilson can be credited for his treatment of secularization as a complex phenomenon involving several separate but interrelated parts. But he also can be criticized for his failure to distinguish the different processes involved in secularization.

A more systematic treatment of secularization is advanced by David Martin in *A General Theory of Secularization* (1978). According to Martin (1978:69), differentiation and "the onset of anomie" are the basic processes related to secularization. These processes are subject to cultural and historical variation, resulting in a variety of basic patterns of secularization. In order to systematize the variations, Martin specifies a series of cultural frames, events, and categories which characterize the basic patterns of secularization. Basic patterns of secularization may be indicated, for example, by the degree of religious pluralism in a society, the degree of anti-clericism, the degree of cultic partcipation, and by other variables relating to structural differentiation (Martin, 1978:59). By evaluating societies according to each indicator, a complex pattern of secularization emerges which is far more detailed and specific than Wilson's general use of the term secularization could provide. Martin is the one contemporary theorist who has made the greatest effort to conceptualize secularization as a complex phenomenon affected by numerous variables and observable in a variety of cultural patterns. He is exceptional in his precise treatment of secularization. In the following analyses of the theories of Durkheim, Weber, Wach, Berger and Luckmann, Wilson, Fenn, and Martin, specific terms such as differentiation and rationalization (desacralization) are substituted whenever possible for the more general term "secularization." This precise delineation of the specific processes associated with secularization will lead to a clearer understanding of patterns of religious evolution and the implications of these patterns for civil religious evolution.

C. Selected Theories of Religious Evolution

1. Emile Durkheim

Durkheim has proposed a unilinear, evolutionary model for the explanation of the religious changes associated with industrial development. The model posits a unilinear movement of societies from the sacred to the profane polarity associated with the process of differentiation. Any examination of Durkheim's model begins with his primary postulate asserting that collective representations, the concrete symbols of the social group, constitute collective reality. The original collective representation, the religious symbol, is the basis from which all other representations evolve (Durkheim, 1912/1926:10). Durkheim further posits a transition in the collective representations from sacred to profane, paralleled by a shift from repressive to restitutive law. From these postulated changes in the collective indicators of social reality, a core Durkheimian hypothesis can be deduced, the movement from mechanical to organic solidarity. In terms of social organization, the transition occurs from segmental to organized social types. The segmental type, analogous to the homogeneous rings of an earthworm, is the social organization of the clan. The organized type, the product of the division of labor, is similar to a "system of different organs each of which has a special role, and which are themselves formed of differentiated parts" (Durkheim, 1893/1933:181). The division of labor itself is causally linked with the growth of moral and material density. Not mere population growth alone, but the increased clustering and interaction of populations are the stimuli setting off a complex chain reaction. Viewed historically, the material and moral density of society induced a division of labor, which produced organized societal types from segmental ones, and organic solidarity from mechanical solidarity. These processes of transition are indicated empirically by the concrete changes in legal sanctions from repressive to restitutive forms, and the movement from sacred to profane collective representations. In highly simplified terms, structural differentiation produces movement from a sacred to a secular society.

Unlike modern privatists, Durkehim does not predict that the common conscience disappears under organic solidarity in modern society. As society becomes more heterogeneous and differentiated, the common conscience would necessarily broaden to include individual differences. Durkheim spent a portion of his intellectual life shifting back and forth on the issue of moral crisis under organic solidarity. On the one hand, he feared the breakdown of the moral community into a state of anomie. On the other, he offered solutions to combat anomie and explanations for the perseverance of morality. One explanation was the evolution of the highest form of morality in organic society with individualism the last surviving mechanical form. According to Bellah (1973:xl-xli) the civil religion Durkheim envisioned for France was based on a combination of justice and rational individualism.

Durkheim's model of religious change can be categorized as a unilinear model of progressive evolution from sacred to profane symbols. The sacred and profane stages are posed as polar opposites, with no intermediary stages defined. Although Durkheim clearly associates the sacred to profane transition with the process of differentiation, users of the model have no clear indicators of the state of sacred beliefs at any given point in time, other than through the empirical examination of restitutive law and of the sacred belief systems themselves. Durkheim's model is therefore quite general and suffers from lack of specification of independent, dependent, and intervening variables. Durkheim's assumption of unilinear diffentiation might also be questioned by the observers of complex social reality. Nevertheless, Durkheim's model stimulated a series of linear theories of religious evolution including those of Wach (1944), Parsons (1971), and Bellah (1964). All of these more clearly specify some of the variables suggested by Durkheim, and critically readdress the assumptions of evolutionary thought. Coleman's (1970) theory of civil religious evolution also is partially derived from Durkheim's general model of cultural and religious evolution.

2. Max Weber

Weber is well-known for his study of religious change in the modern industrial period (Weber, 1905). Weber's concept for the unilinear process of modernization is rationalization, a process which has important implications for religious systems. Through increasing use of rational bases for human social action, the world gradually loses its sacred character to causal and efficiency-oriented explanations of reality. Rationality refers to the functional rationality in which goal attainment is based on utilitarian principles. The effect of rationalization of religion is secularizaton of the "desacralization of the world" type (Shiner, 1968:215-216). In the religious sphere, the trend of progressive rationalization is evidenced in the social attitude of "disenchantment."

Weber's study of the Protestant Ethic is an effort to gauge the effects of progressive rationalization in the context of modern Protestantism. In particular, Weber was interested in the legitimating function of religion, and how that function might be affected by rationalization. His conclusions on the Protestant Ethic thesis have been controversial and open to varying interpretations and critiques. One commentator, David Little (1970) has made observations having particular relevance to the relationship between rationalization and system of legitimation. According to Little's analysis of Weber, rationalization and the rational-legal type of authority assume increasing institutional differentiation and autonomy, in contrast to the institutional dominance of the traditional system. Yet, religion always serves as a legitimating force, even for the process of rationalization. Rationalization is legitimized by the ultimate values of a culture, which have religious significance. Little concludes that Weber found Calvinism and Puritanism to be congruent in their support of the capitalist ethos, and thus served as legitimating factors (1970:13). Although neither Weber nor Little addresses the issue of civil religion, Little's interpretation of Weber's theory of modernization is congruent with Coleman's theory of civil religious evolution. Both theories predict increasing differentiation as the basic evolutionary process. Both theories also state that the crisis of order precipitated by differentiation must be addressed by an ultimate system of reference. For Coleman, this ultimate system of reference is civil religion.

3. Joachim Wach

Wach's (1944) historical model of religious change contains many descriptive examples of the ways in which religious differentiation follows social differentiation. The result is somewhat similar to Bellah's (1964) differentiation theory of religious evolution (see figure 1). Wach's model outlines three types, or stages, of church-state relationship. In the primitive Stage 1, church and state are fused to the point that it is impossible to determine which institution dominates. In Stage 2 (comparable to Bellah's archaic and historic religions) both politics and cults gain strength, leading either to state establishment as a means of control over religion, or the beginnings of the process of eventual church-state separation. In Stage 3 (Bellah's historic, early modern, and modern religions) the state reacts to new and competing religions with the same alternatives of Stage 2 — establshment or pluralism (Wach, 1944:299:302).Wach's model does not address the possibilities subsequently raised by Coleman (1970) for the variation of church-state relations in contemporary societies.

While Wach's linear model of religious change is not terribly sophisticated, it sets the style of future, more elaborate models developed by Parsons (1971) and Bellah (1964). Wach's treatment of religious evolution is to be credited for its analysis of secularization in terms of the more specific processes of social and religious differentiation. In Wach's view, differentiation and the resulting pluralization of religious structures, not secularization, are the characteristic and dominant processes of the modern age. That civil religious systems follow the same differentiating pattern as other religious systems, is a logical extension of Wach's model to the realm of civil religion.

4. Peter Berger and Thomas Luckmann

The works of Peter Berger and Thomas Luckmann on religion and modernization will be examined together, based on their collaboration in the development of the dialectical process theory presented in *The Social Construction of Reality* (1966). The dialectical process theory traces the mechanisms by which social forms are "internalized" through socialization, "externalized" through social action, and "objectified" through reification and institutionalization, only to be internalized by the subsequent generation. Through this on-going dialectical process, social reality (including religious reality) is "created."

Peter Berger (1967) views religion as the human construction of a "sacred cosmos" (1967:25). During the dialectic stage of objectification, religious constructions are reified and become separated from the individual. When religious constructions begin to lose their power, due to industralization,cultural differentiation, or other forces inherent in religion itself, secularization emerges in a similar dialectical process. Berger views secularization as both a societal and an individual process. On the social level, secularization is the process by which religions lose their legitimating influence over segments of society. This conception of secularization is similar to Shiner's (1968:212-214) "disengagement of society from religion." Secularization of consciousness refers to the individual loss of religious interpretations of the world and of the self. Through secularization, religion, no longer the source of binding worldview and moral community, becomes privatized. In one sense, secularization (differentiation) has acted as a disorganizing process. But it also has created a world of many religious and nonreligious modes of potential reorganization.

Although Peter Berger does not use the term "American civil religion," in *The Noise of Solemn Assemblies* (1961:39;75) he describes forms of American "cultural religion" and "political religion." Cultural and political religion are potential manifestations of American civil religion conceived as folk religion. Cultural religion is based on the commonly shared American values of this-worldliness, succes, activism, and social adjustment, (Berger, 1961:42-46) and functions to promote social integration. Political religion, the manifestation of cultural religion within the polity, performs the additional function of social control (Berger, 1961:71-72). Berger's vision of American civil religion is similar to the religion-in-general of Marty and Herberg. In Berger's view, American civil religion is necessarily highly generalized in order to overarch denominational pluralism and church-state separation. Berger does not recognize a transcendent aspect of American civil religion. Instead, he depicts a folk religion performing an essentially conservative function (Berger, 19961:52). According to Berger's theory, the process of secularization in America has produced a civil religion that is more of a national ideology than a transcendent religion.

Thomas Luckmann (1967) focuses more specifically than Berger upon the reorganization potential of secularization for religion. Luckmann's 1967 analysis begins by noting that the sociology of religion frequently has assumed that church and religion are identical. This assumption leads to the conclusion that when modernization began to undermine the traditional churches, religion was similarly undermined. Luckmann suggests that the study of the effects of modernization on existing religious institutions actually obscures the fact that new religious meaning systems are being developed (1967:40).

Luckmann describes several alternative modes of adaptation to the erosion of traditional religious meanings. The individual alternatively may make an individualistic "leap of faith" into a personal, religious meaning system. He or she may shift back and forth between traditional and secular definitions of reality. Finally,he or she may develop an explicitly secular value system (1967:86). Church religion is thus one surviving organizational form of religion, and is not disorganized in the formal organizational sense of the term. Private, but still religious, views of reality are also emerging, based (according to Luckmann) on the themes of autonomy, self-expression, self-realization, the mobility ethos, sexuality, and familism (1967:108-114). These themes are later repeated by Richard Fenn (1972:17). Luckmann is also in agreement with Fenn (1970;1972;1974) in concluding that the new, subjective religious forms are far less cohesive than traditional religious forms, and have a low degree of transcendence. The evolutionary perspective is maintained in Luckmann's prediction that the religious trends he describes are irreversible by-products of modern industrialism.

Neither Berger nor Luckmann specifies stages of religious evolution associated with stages of modernization. Differentiation and its impact on religious construction of reality proceeds in an unspecified evolutionary manner, marked only the dialectical process stages of objectification, externalization, and internalization. While neither Berger nor Luckmann deals explicitly with the functions of religion, both generally predict a decline of the role of traditional religion in fostering social integration and legitimation of meaning. Both predict a weakening of traditional religious structures, the privatization of religion, and the development of multiple sacred and secular ideological choices for the modern individual. Although Berger and Luckmann do not include transcendent civil religion as one of the possible religious choices in contemporary society, presumably civil religion could provide an alternative mode of adaptation to the erosion of traditional religion. The fact that neither theorist considers civil religion for this purpose suggests that privatism does not offer strong support for the evolution of civil religions.

5. Bryan Wilson

Wilson draws upon Durkheim's asumption of unilinear differentiation and Weber's process of rationalization. The modern theory of secularization characterizes religion as declining in influence, becoming desacralized, and differentiated from other institutions due to the advent of industrialization and technological development. The result is that "traditional theology, church organization, and sacred rituals appear to be fundamentally irreconcilable with the values, lifestyles, and functional imperatives of advanced industrial society" (Wilson, 1968:73). Sources of the decline of religion are found in the processes of differentiation and rationalization, particularly in "the decline of community," "increased social mobility," and "the impersonality of role relationships" (Wilson, 1976:-99). Where these processes are observable, as in Western societies, societal responses include ecumenism, voluntary destructuration, incorporation of rationalization, eclecticism, and charismatic renewal (Wilson, 1976:85).These responses to religious erosion are all viewed as manifestations of the overriding process of secularization.Even counter-secular forces such as religious renewal are characterized as merely ephemeral substitutes for the declining traditional religous organizations.

Although Wilson posits the erosion of religious beliefs and institutions along a line of progressive rationalization, he is aware of cultural and historical variation in religious evolution. The unique feature affecting the American pattern of religious evolution has been the structure of denominational pluralism. Wilson believes that the American pattern of interdenominational competition is but a religious manifestation of a major American secular value; competition. As a result, American churches become voluntary associations held together primarily by their social function. In Wilson's (1968:79) view, religious organizations in America function as "surrogate communities based on the will for togetherness," performing emotional functions for individuals, but failing to provide sources of societal legitimation and regulation.

Although Wilson limits his own analysis to denominational religion, his theory of the progressive decline of religion in modern society has implications for the study of American civil religion. Wilson's asumption of unilinear religious decline and desacralization leads to a privatistic position. He concludes that religious cohesion (and by implication, civil religious cohesion) is lost in the rationalized, differentiated society. New religious movements are dismissed as too transitory and uninstitutionalized to provide new bases of societal integration and legitimacy. The potential of civil religion to perform these functions is not even considered. Application of Wilson's assumptions to American civil religion would lead to the conclusion that American civil religion, like other religious forms, has declined in influence. If American civil religion persists at all, it would be manifest as a nationally self-transcendent folk religion.

Wilson's theory is limited by the assumption of unilinear secularization. Once secularization is predicted, all observable religious forms are necessarily viewed as eroding, inadequate, or transitory. The persistence of religious symbols and the phenomenon of religious renewal are not adequately explained. Additionally, Wilson's assumptions lead to the prediction of a societal crisis. He (1976:114-115) warns that "no persisting society can leave people to do their own thing" and observes that "we know no moral order to give meaning to our social order." If these statements are accurate, presumably modern society no longer exists! Obviously, modern social orders do persist. Wilson fails to confront this evidence and is drawn into a contradiction, which could be addressed by recognizing civil religion as a potential source of social cohesion and legitimation for modern society.

6. Richard Fenn

In a recent work, *Toward a Theory of Secularization* (1978), Fenn locates the evolution of civil religion within the general context of religious evolution by specifying the emergence and subsequent decline of civil religion as one stage of a secularization process (differentiation). The five steps in Fenn's theory of secularization are:

Step 1	Differentiation of religious roles and institutions. *Differentiation may be partial, continuing and reversible.
Step 2	Demand for clarification of boundary between religious and secular issues. *Conflict between religious ethnic groups and the larger society.
Step 3	Development of generalized religious symbols or ideology: the "civil religion." *Problems of authenticity arise in the political use of religious themes.
Step 4	Minority and idiosyncratic definitions-of-the-situation: secularized political authority. *The dispersion of the sacred.
Step 5	The separation of individual from corporate life. *Religious groups differ in their conceptions of the scope of the sacred and in their demands for integration of corporate and personal values systems (Fenn, 1978:xvii).

Fenn predicts that civil religion will emerge as a societal solution by transcending particularistic ethnic and religious identities that divide society. Civil religion is a socially constructed myth, which is more or less believable depending upon societal, and particularly political, conditions. For example, the power of civil religion is weakened when political or economically motivated activity is masked by the symbols of civil religion. The symbols become tarnished and lose their transcendent, unifying potential. In the final stages of secularization, the state loses its sacred character, while "a wider range of personal and social activity comes to acquire sacred significance." Ultimately, the boundary between secular and sacred realms corresponds to the boundary between societal and personality systems (Fenn, 1978:54).

Fenn (1978:53) acknowledges that his theory of religious evolution leads toward a "death of society" position. Unlike Wilson, Fenn is willing to confront this issue by questioning the process by which sociologists infer that a morally based social order exists. In Fenn's (1978:ix) view, such inferences are forms of "mystification" and "idolatry" and are inappropriate perspectives from which to conduct sociological inquiry. Although Fenn's five steps lead toward the moral dissolution of society, the trend is not portrayed as unilinear. There is a dynamic tension between the trend toward desacralization of the societal system and the contrary trend of "desecularization" in other areas of social life. As the state is demythologized, private religious mythologies become more demanding and competitive (Fenn, 1978:55). By recognizing the dynamic relationship between secularization and desecularization, Fenn acknowledges that religious change is a complex process manifest through seemingly paradoxical trends and counter-trends. Fenn remains closed, however, to the possbility of desecularization at the societal level leading to the renewal of American civil religion. "To establish the existence of such a cultural whole inevitably requires a leap beyond the data" (Fenn, 1978:51). Although Fenn is only willing to discuss American civil religion in the *past* tense, the fact that he includes civil religion as a critical phase of religious evolution is a contribution to the study of the relationship between general religious trends and patterns of civil religious evolution.

7. David Martin

In *A General Theory of Secularization* (1978) David Martin outlines a series of propositions designed to specify the conditions under which religious institutions lose influence and religious beliefs become desacralized. The resulting theory is more specific and complex than the other theories surveyed here because more than one basic pattern of secularizaton is proposed. Differentiation is specified as the major universal process affecting religious change in modern societies. Martin is careful to note that, although universal processes may be expected to occur, they are not invariate and are subject to influence from a number of cultural factors. Cultural "frames" through which differentiation flows include major historical events, such as the Reformation or the American Revolution; the influence of major ideologies, such as Calvinism or enlightenment thought; and the relationship between religion and cultural identity (Martin, 1978:4-9). These general cultural frames suggest additional categories of variables Martin isolates as particularly crucial to the formation of basic patterns of secularization. Major categories include: (1) whether the society is Catholic or not; (2) whether the religion is monopolistic or not; and (3) whether the society has developed through internal conflict or conflict against external oppressors (Martin, 1978:17). Variations in these categories result in the basic patterns of secularization observable in different societies. Although Martin (1978:59) considers as many as eight different patterns of secularization, the dominant types are the Anglo-Saxon, American, French, and Russian patterns. Martin suggests a number of additional characteristics by which the basic patterns can be identified and better understood. Basic patterns of secularization may vary according to many factors including the degree of anti-clericism, the status of the clergy, the degree of cultic participation, the influence of intellectualism in religion, the extent of democratic or communist influence, the existence of religious political parties, and the type of civil religion (Martin, 1978:59).

Martin's complex scheme may be illustrated by examination of one of the four major patterns of secularization — the American case. According to Martin, the American pattern of secularization was framed in a pluralistic, Protestant society which was strongly shaped in a revolution against foreign rule. The result is a society where church and state are differentiated, where denominations and sects have proliferated and command large memberships, and where religious organizations play an important role in the sponsorship of charitabable and welfare endeavors. The clergy, however, lack social power and are "assimilated to the concept of rival entrepreneurs running varied religious services on a mixed laissez-faire and oligopolistic model." American religious organizations remain influential on some measurements (membership and professed belief) and show decline on others (social power, maintenance of theological rigor). Unlike Bryan Wilson, Martin does not portray secularization as an absolute trend. Differentiation, as framed by the unique American cultural configuration, has produced a mixture of secular and religious forms. Individual response to secularization is also complex. Personal responses to the differentiation of American society include: (1) apathy accompanied by withdrawal from institutional religion; (2) a turn to mysticism as a reaction against fragmentation and meaninglessness; and (3) a search for functional equivalents to religion in the family, community, or commune (Martin, 1978:93). Within American culture a religious cycle of response to differentiation can be detected. (1978:31). Martin's propositions lead to a theory of religious evolution in America which incorporates both linear and cyclical change.

A central feature of the complex pattern of American religious evolution as characterized by Martin is the existence of American civil religion (1978:28). Martin views American civil religion as a by-product of the American cultural frame of church-state separation, the synthesis of Protestantism and enlightenment thought, and the Revolutionary experience of internal cohesion against external domination. Like Robert Bellah (1975),Martin locates the historical origins of American civil religion in the fusion of Puritan and Enlightenment principles of the American founders, which led to the institutionalization of church-state separation. Because no monopoly religion existed, the moral basis of the social order was necessarily derived from general values which could overarch particular religious organizations (1978:70).

In Parsonian terms, differentiation is accompanied by value generalization (Parsons, 1971). Martin is aware of both the structural strengths and weaknesses of American civil religion. The fact that the values of American civil religion must be highly general to unite a pluralistic society is not necessarily a weakness. "If an ideal is sufficiently broad, it cannot be compromised by poor political performance and corruption, but acts rather as a potent point of moral appeal" (Martin, 1978:70). A typical response to the Watergate scandal, for example, was the isolation of Richard Nixon as an immoral individual rather than the total condemnation of American standards of political morality. Yet, Richard Fenn (1978) has warned that the symbols of American civil religion are vulnerable to manipulation for political and economic goals, with loss of public faith a common result. Martin also acknowledges this structural problem, but predicts that if the vision of American civil religion remains future oriented, the covenant is less likely to be broken. Martin's portrayal of American civil religion recalls Bellah's (1975) image of the broken covenant. American civil religion is seen as constituting a generalized system of national legitimation, cohesion, and prophecy, which under specific conditions can fail at one or all of these areas of performance. Variations in the performance of American civil religion are not automatically viewed by Martin as evidence of the death of American society.

Martin's theory of religious evolution begins where many of the other theories cited in this chapter terminate, with the processes of differentiation and rationalization of modern society. Instead of assuming that these modern trends proceed invariably to a universal decline of religion, Martin probes for sources of cultural variation which shape religious change. Martin provides a theoretical framework by which variations in religious evolution may be studied empirically. Martin's approach differs from that of such unilinear theorists as Bryan Wilson, who tends to interpret all behavior as manifestations of secularization once secularization has been assumed.

However, Martin's theory also has limitations. Some of his variables overlap with one another. He is unclear about the number of basic patterns of secularization to be specified. He fails to distinguish clearly independent from dependent variables. Despite these limitations, Martin has developed a general theory of religious change accounting for a variety of cross-cultural religious patterns, as well as the specific patterns of religious evolution within a single society. When Martin's theory is applied to the United States, a number of religious and "secular" phenomena are revealed, including the presence of American civil religion. American civil religion is portrayed as the religious symbol system of the nation subject to the same evolutionary influences and shaped by the same cultural frame as other American religious forms. By viewing civil religion as one variable in the context of religious change, Martin contributes perspective to the study of both religious evolution and American civil religion.

8. A Summary and Evaluation of the Theories of Religious Evolution

Among the theories of religious change considered here, religious evolution has been variously conceived of as occurring unilinearly between two discrete poles (Durkheim), along the progressive line of rationalization (Weber and Wilson), along a continuum of cultural and religious differentiation (Wach and Fenn), in a dialectical process of social reality construction (Berger and Luckmann), and as a complex combination of linear and cyclical processes within cultural frames (Martin). S. N. Eisenstadt (1964:375) notes that two critical stumbling blocks for evolutionary models have been the assumption of linearity and the failure to fully specify the systematic characteristics of major develomental stages. The models of Durkheim, Weber, Wach and Wilson are limited, in differing degrees, by assumed linearity. Among the linear theorists only Fenn (1978) is careful to note that his model is not dependent upon the absolute linearity of differentiation. Martin's model, which accounts for both linear and cyclic trends, does not assume that universal trends such as differentiation always occur (Martin, 1978:3). The dialectical model of Berger and Luckmann has been included for discussion primarily because it does not maintain a linear perspective. The models of Durkheim, Weber, Wach, Berger and Luckmann, Wilson, and Fenn are also limited by their failure to specify the defining systemic characteristics of evolutionary stages. Martin presents defining categories for the basic patterns of secularization with reliance upon an explicitly historical evolutionary sequence. Of the two criteria for useful evolutionary models noted by Eisenstadt, avoidance of rigid linear assumptions and specificaton of systemic characteristics,only Martin's model meets both criteria.

The models of Durkheim, Weber, and Wach serve as intellectual predecessors of the Parsonian evolutionary model, elaborated and adapted by Bellah and Coleman. The classic theories of religious change advanced by Durkheim, Weber, and Wach are highly congruent with Coleman's (1970) elaboration of civil religious change. Coleman's theory specifies types of civil religious manifestations, based on the level of differentiation within a society. Coleman finds religion, civil religion, and political systems generally undifferentiated in primitive and archaic societies. Civil religious systems may gradually begin to differentiate in historical or early modern societies, but do not appear in differentiated form until the modern period. Coleman believes that the pattern of a completely differentiated civil religion is evident only in the United States. His theory can be summarized by adding a third proposition to the two propositions previously advanced in Chapter 4.

Proposition III: The differentiation of American civil religion from religious and political institutions follows the general direction of cultural evolution.

Proposition III proposes nothing new for the sociology of religion beyond inclusion of the concept of civil religious evolution as an aspect of religious evolution under the specific condition of social differentiation. Additional variables and cultural configurations affecting civil religion are suggested by Martin's contemporary secularization theory. The Berger and Luckmann dialectic model does not directly contradict the proposition, but neither does it provide a supportive framework. Berger and Luckmann take a privatistic position, similar to that of Bryan Wilson and Richard Fenn, all of which forsee traditional religious systems losing significance for modern society. Neither Berger and Luckmann, Wilson, nor Fenn would predict the evolution of any overarching religious symbol system, including civil religion, in modern societies. Proposition III and the two preceding propositions concerning American civil religion receive their greatest support from Durkheimian and Parsonian evolutionary thought, and the least support from modern privatism. Those contemporary theorists offering the strongest conceptual framework for the study of the evolution of civil religion are Martin, Bellah and Coleman.

CHAPTER 6
APPLICATIONS

A. Introduction

We have proposed that the differentiation of American civil religion from religious and political institutions follows the general direction of cultural evolution. This proposition implies that cultural variation in civil religious forms is dependent upon the degree of differentiation in the society. Cross-cultural applications are presented next in order to highlight American civil religion by contrasting it with other types of civil religion. The American case is examined in further detail first, then compared to civil reigion in modern Great Britain, Restoration Japan, and the Soviet Union. Comparison of the four civil religious forms, supplemented by data from a cross-cultural empirical study of civil religion by Cole and Hammond (1974), suggest that civil religious types vary cross-culturally according to the degree of differentiation and religious pluralism within the society.

B. The American Case

1. Cole and Hammond

John A. Coleman (1970) has proposed three types of civil religion in modern societies: (1) continued undifferentiated civil religion, either church or state sponsored, (2) secular nationalism, and (3) differentiated civil religion. Coleman believes the third type, differentiated civil religion, is observable only in the United States. In a highly differentiated society, civil religion tends to follow the pattern of differentiation and move away from either political or religious sponsorship. In a religiously plural society there is no need for the functions of civil religion to be performed by a secular version of nationalism. The historical strength of the American religious tradition, combined with the absence of religious establishment, set the stage for the differentiation of a religiously oriented, but non-church-sponsored, civil religious system. Thus far, theory and research have been presented to support the thesis of a differentiated civil religion in the United States. Most significant are Wimberley's (1976) empirical findings that a measurable civil religious dimension of belief is distinguishable from either religious or political belief systems. Coleman's theory would predict that Wimberley's findings of a differentiated civil religion are unique to the United States. Cross-cultural empirical research by Cole and Hammond (1974) points to a similar conclusion. It is Hammond's (1974) thesis that in modern, religiously plural societies, the function of societal conflict resolution moves away from the domain of traditional religion and comes under the control of legal institutions. The legal structures of modern society become the new source of moral integration. In Cole and Hammond's research this hypothesis is tested. The major variables, examined for ninety-two nations, were religious pluralism, societal complexity, and legal development. Religious pluralism, measured by the number of religious groups comprising at least 2 percent of a society's population, was expected to be related to the level of societal complexity, measured by indicators of levels of communication, technology, bureaucratic organization, and money and market complex. Both pluralism and societal complexity were expected to be related to degree of legal develoment, measured by the extent of legal repression. Evidence of repression signified that legal development was low, while absence of repressive laws indicated a higher level of legal development (Cole and Hammond, 1974:181-183).

These data also indicated a positive relationship between legal development and societal complexity. Although religious pluralism is a type of societal complexity, it was found to have (as predicted) an inhibiting effect on "secular" or economic indicators of complexity. These data also indicated a positive relationship between legal development and societal complexity. Societies with the highest levels of legal development were the most complex. Additionally, these data revealed that as religious pluralism increases, the positive association between societal complexity and legal development also increases. Figure 8 illustrates the findings. Substituting the terms used in Propositions I through III for the terms used by Cole and Hammond, the relationships also could be diagrammed as they appear in figure 9.

Figure 8
Relationship between Religious Pluralism, Societal Complexity, and Legal Development (Cole and Hammond, 1974)

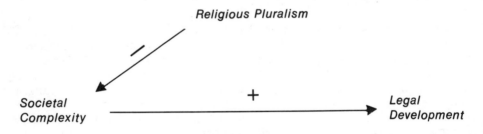

Figure 9
Hypothesized Relationship between Religious Pluralism, Institutional Differentiation, and Differentiated Civil Religion

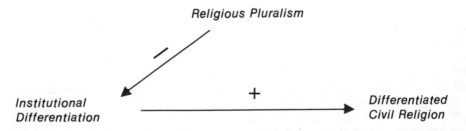

Cole and Hammond apply their findings to the issue of civil religious development and suggest that in a religiously plural society conflict can be generated through a clash of religious meaning systems (1974:186). If the conflict is to be resolved, some overarchng system of meaning must develop which can integrate the conflicting systems. If this overarching system of integration, the legal system, adopts universal language and acts to legitimate behavior as well as to resolve conflict, it constitutes a system of civil religion. Cole and Hammond expect most plural, complex and legally developed nations to feature civil religious orientations in their legal systems. The United States, although not included in the sample of nations, is singled out as the society most likely to exhibit civil religious symbols in its legal order, (1974:187).

Other nations ranking high in societal complexity, religious pluralism, and legal development (e.g., Bulgaria, Malay, the Philippines, and Trinidad) are treated as developing nations whose level of civil religious development should be reflected in their legal systems. Cole and Hammond do not consider their findings to be conclusive but suggest that civil religious development is a cross-cultural, observable, evolutionary phenomenon, related to other indices of societal development. The clearest indicator of civil religious development today may be found in the legal system of the societies under study.

2. American Civil Religion and Judicial System;

Cole and Hammond's study points to legal systems as institutional carriers of civil religion. Although in all societies the legal order is an arm of the state, in the United States the governmental structure of checks and balances results in a judicial system semi-autonomous from the legislative and executive branches. While officials in the judicial system are appointed by executives to rule on laws enacted by legislators, judicial officials also have the power to declare laws unconstitutional, and to judge elected officials for legal offenses. To the extent that the judicial system can override decisions made in other governmental systems, the judicial system may be seen as partially differentiated from other branches of the state. In the United States the judiciary has the autonomy to take a prophetic stance with regard to other political and social institutions.

Hammond hypothesizes that the American system of religious pluralism is the key variable contributing to the expansion of judicial influence in the United States. In a religiously plural society, the judiciary is required to maintain order and develop universally acceptable explanations for legal decisions. With the expansion of the judicial system, "the judiciary has adapted the task of articulating the collective moral architecture" (Hammond, 1974:129).Hammond discusses several United State Supreme Court cases which illustrate civil religion as a product of the judicial system. The cases noted by Hammond all concern issues of church-state separation, a major legal arena in which the society's commitment to religious pluralism has been tested.

In *Church of the Holy Trinity v. United States,* 143 U.S. 226 (1892), the "moral architecture" constructed by the Court reflected the Protestant civic piety of the nineteenth century. The Court held that a law prohibiting the importation of aliens for labor did not prevent a church from hiring a foreign minister. The Court affirmed that "we are a Christian people, and the morality of the country is deeply ingrafted upon Christianity" (quoted in Hammond, 1974:139). By the time of *United States v. Macintosh, 283 U.S.05 (1931),* the Court had developed a separationist position with regard to church and state. The Court was asked to decide if citizenship should be denied to a person unwilling to fight in the nation's defense. Although the Court acknowledged the right of freedom of religious belief, it held that the nation's goal of survival was primary. Citizenship was denied, justified by the ultimate objective of national survival. In two subsequent conscientious objector cases, *United States v. Seeger,* 380 U.S. 163 (1965) and *Welsh v. United States,* 398 U.S. 333 (1970), the Court broadened the concept of religious belief to include views other than orthodox monotheistic beliefs. Both Seeger and Welsh were granted conscientious objector status on the basis of "moral, ethical or religious beliefs about what is right or wrong" (quoted in Hammond, 1974:131). The *Welsh* decision affirmed that in a religiously plural society an individual's *own* perception of his or her beliefs as religious was of prime importance in the Court's recognition of them as religious. With the *Seeger* and *Welsh* decisions, " 'religion' for legal purposes becomes simply 'conscience' " (Hammond, 1974:132).The multiplication of religious definitions within society required the Supreme Court to redefine religion in a way to reduce religious conflict and foster social integration. The authority to make decisions on issues of ultimacy as they affect the naton illustrates Hammond's thesis that the courts are the architects of "common religion" or "civil religion" (Hammond, 1974:133-134).

Legal scholar Robert McCloskey(1972) agrees with Hammond that both the structure and ethical influence of the United States Supreme Court have expanded in the past forty years, beginning with the period of the Stone Court (1940:1945) established after the New Deal. Most of the major Court decisions restricting the role of religion in the public schools (see figure 7) occurred during the 1940s, 1950s, and 1960s. Americans have learned to expect the Court to perform the dual functions of interpreting the law and applying the law fairly and ethically to the issue under consideration. The expectation for ethical judgements by the Court does not imply that all Americans agree with the ethical outcomes of judicial decisions, or that all Americans even support the judiciary's right to render such decisions. Public protest of the *Engle* (1962) and *Schempp* (1963) decisions declaring public school-sponsored prayer and devotional Bible reading uncontitutional was widespread. Segments of the public were also outraged at the desegregation decision in *Brown v. Board or Education,* 347 U.S. 483 (1954). *Goldstein v. Collin,* 99 U.S. 277 (1976), in which the Court ruled that an American Nazi group could demonstrate publicly in a community with a large Jewish population, is a recent example of a judicial decision which aroused public criticism on a national scale. McCloskey suggests that public reaction to a judicial decision is often confused due to the failure to distinguish between the differing functions of the courts (1972:292). The very fact that judicial decisions are often unpopular with the public suggests that the ethical function of the judiciary becomes at times a prophetic rather than a priestly expression of the values of American civil religion.

There are numerous foci of modern Court decisions that illustrate the civil religious functions of the judiciary. The separation of church and state issue explored by Hammond (1974) and the issue of religion in the public schools, discussed in chapter four, both directly addressed the society's role with regard to multiple definitions of ultimate reality. The civil rights decisions, such as *Brown,* evoked the ethical principle of fairness while interpreting the law to protect the rights of minority citizens. Less obvious in their civil religous implications, but no less relevant, are judicial decisions concerned with the civil religious values of individual freedom and social equality. A recent illustrative example is the United States Supreme Court decision on the death penalty in *Furman v. Georgia,* 408 U.S. 238 (1972).

Furman concerned two ethical issues, the right of the state to impose the death penalty and the equal application of punishment. The three defendants in the case, who had received death sentences, appealed their cases to the Supreme Court arguing that the death penalty constituted "cruel and unusual punishment" and therefore violated the Eighth Amendment of the Constitution. While the Court refused to rule that capital punishment *per se* is cruel and unusual, it did rule that the death penalty was unconstitutional in these three cases because its imposition constituted racial discrimination. Justice Brennan, in a concurring opinion, attempted to define "cruel and unusual" punishment. He states that the Court cannot define "cruel and unusual" punishment in general, but must instead decide each case of punishment to determine if it is cruel and unusual. Constitutional guidelines for evaluation of punishments are based on three fundamental principles: that (1) "even the vilest criminal remains a human being possessed of common dignity;" (2) "the State must not arbitrarily inflict a severe punishment;" and (3) "a severe punishment must not be unacceptable to contemporary society" (*Furman v. Georgia,* 1972:272-286).The civil religious nature of the three principles is self-evident, as the principles directly concern the American civil religious values of human dignity and social equality. The final guiding principle of the Court evaluates the society and its moral consensus as the final arbitrator of the life or death of its citizens. Subsequently, in *Gregg v. Georgia,* 96 S.Ct. 2909 (1976), the Court went a step beyond *Furman* to decide that capital punishment is not invariably unconstitutional, leaving the way open for state legislators to develop acceptable death penalty statutes. The *Furman* and *Gregg* decisions demonstrate the Supreme Court's active role in constructing the moral architecture of the nation.

Several examples have been selected from United States Supreme Court cases to illustrate Hammond's (1974) thesis that interpretation of the law has civil religious implications. The judicial decisions chosen as examples are by no means randomly selected. Contrary decisions on similar issues could be found. However, the direction of judicial decisions, or the popularity of such decisions, are irrelevant to their consideration as civil religions. Whether the courts rule that capital punishment is or is not unconstitutional, the courts are addressing an ethical issue's ultimate implications for state and citizen. In the United States, the judicial system is in a unique position with regard to the legitimation of civil religious values. The rhetoric of American civil religion can be found outside the courtroom, in politicians' speeches or clergymen's sermons, but nowhere outside the courtroom does the rhetoric of American civil religion have such binding moral and legal force. Hammond questions the relationship between the generalized American civil religion espoused in other social institutions and the more particularistic moral architecture constructed by the courts. Hammond (1974:155) asks "How does 'God', as portrayed in Presidential speech, relate to due process, as portrayed in Supreme Court opinion?"

An answer to Hammond's question is suggested by Propositions I through III and Coleman's thesis of a *differentiated* civil religion in the United States. If American religion is particularly formulated and legitimated by the judicial system in the United States, then American civil religion is not entirely differentiated from the state. It is semi-differentiated to the extent that the judiciary is itself semi-differentiated from other governmental institutions. Obviously, further examination of the role performed by the American judicial system is required in conjunction with study of the evolution of American civil religion.

3. Summary

Coleman (1970) proposes that under conditions of institutional differentiation and religious pluralism, a differentiated form of civil religion will develop. Cole and Hammond (1974) present cross-cultural data suggesting that the conditions necessary for the development of civil religion are, the absence of a universally established religion, religious pluralism, and high levels of societal and legal complexity. American society meets these criteria, and therefore is one in which *differentiated civil religion* would be expected to develop. Cole and Hammond predict that the conflict resolution function of a society's legal system will serve as an important indicator of the differentiation of civil religion. Examination of the American legal system, particularly the judiciary, reveals numerous examples of conflict resolution legitimated by what Bellah (1975) defines as civil religious ideals. If Hammond's thesis is correct, the most value-specific source of American civil religion is the judicial system, where Hammond believes the "not-so-elementary forms" of American civil religion reside today (Hammond, 1974:135).

C. Cross-Cultural Research

In the preceding discussion, Coleman's theory of the evolution of civil religion was applied to the United States, the society most likely to demonstrate evidence of a *differentiated* civil religion. But what of other modern societies? If the development of civil religion follows the lines of cultural evolution, differentiated civil religion could be expected in other differentiated societies. However, an additional variable intervenes in the evolution of civil religion, the history of church-state relations in the given society. A society may be differentiated, but lacking differentiated civil religion if it lacks a tradition of church-state separation. Great Britain, for example, is a differentiated society, culturally similar to the United States. Yet, the British traditions of an established church and the divine right of kings are manifest today in the retention of a church-sponsored civil religion. State Shintoism in Restoration Japan represents Coleman's other type of continued undifferentiated civil religion: state-sponsored civil religion. The modern U.S.S.R. illustrates the secular alternative to civil religion, *secular nationalism*. The cases of modern Great Britain, Restoration Japan, and the U.S.S.R. are examined as cases of the variation in civil religious evolution in modern and modernizing societies. The three selected cases are presented in some detail because each closely fits the parameters of one of Coleman's basic types of civil religion. Limitation of the discussion to three cases in no way implies that comparable civil religious forms could not be observed in other societies. It is not our intention to present a comprehensive cross-cultural examination of civil religious systems, but to highlight representative types leading to the isolation of key variables affecting civil religious development.

Coleman (1970:70) states that the absence of civil religion should not be assumed merely because a differentiated system of civil religion has not appeared within a society. In the absence of differentiated civil religion, the functions of civil religion may be performed either by a church-sponsored or a state-sponsored type.

1. Church-Sponsored Civil Religion: Modern Great Britain

Civil religion is church-sponsored when an established religious tradition within the society provides the context for sacred civic symbols. Although there are ample examples of church-sponsored civil religion in the non-Christian world (e.g., modern Israel and the Islamic, Khomeini government of Iran), in Great Britain historical Christianity sponsors the symbols of civil religion. The "civil religious concepts of the sacredness of the monarchical form of government in the divine right of kings" and "the notion of the manifest destiny of the Anglo-Saxon nations in the unfolding providence of world history" are British traditions (Coleman, 1970:70). In modern Britain, the monarchy retains little overt political influence, but the ceremonial influence of the monarchy is still pronounced.

In a symbolic study of the British Coronation Service, Edward Shils and Michael Young (1953) present a description of the civil religious functions retained by the modern British monarchy. They (1953:65) base their study of the British Coronation Service on the assumption of the existence of a "general moral consensus of society" founded upon the standards and beliefs of societal members. Common consensual standards in Western societies include generosity, charity, loyalty, justice, respect for authority, dignity of the individual, and the right to individual freedom. These consensual moral values counter individual egotism and provide the basis for a social bond (Shils and Young, 1953:65). The general moral consensus to which Shils and Young refer can be recognized as Bellah's (1976a) concept of *general* civil religion, which provides the religious discipline necessary for responsible moral citizenship and an integrated society. The special expression of moral consensus, or general civil religion, occurs during occasions of national celebration. Ceremonial occasions are important events in a society's life during which societal mores are ritually affirmed and renewed. Shils and Young present a symbolic analysis of the Coronation Service itself, and of the public participation in this civil religious celebration. The focal symbol of the service is the monarch's vow to abide by the moral standards of the society. Each portion of the service reaffirms the monarch's obedience to God and to the Church of England.

The recognition: The presentation of the monarch to the assembly by the Archbishop signifies Church sponsorship of monarchical authority. "When the Archbishop presents the Queen to the four sides of the 'theatre', he is asking the assembly to reaffirm their allegiance to her not so much as an individual as the incumbent of an office of authority" (Shils and Young, 1953:68).

The oath: On taking the oath of office, the monarch promises to govern all British subjects in accordance with the laws of state and the laws of God. By doing this, the monarch acknowledges "the superiority of the transcendent moral standards and their divine source, and therewith the sacred character of the moral standards of British society" (Shils and Young, 1953:68)

Presenting the Holy Bible: The Bible presented to the monarch symbolizes God's law and will, which are to continually inspire the monarch's public decisions. "The Bible is the vessel of God's intention, a source of continuous inspiration in the moral regulation of society" (Shils and Young, 1953:69).

The anointing: The Archbishop anoints the monarch with oil, a symbolic act which sanctifies her assumption of office. The anointing continues a tradition which began with the anointing of King Solomon, and has continued for all British rulers. After the anointing, the monarch "shows her submission before the Archbishop as God's agent, kneeling before him while he implores God to bless her" (Shils and Young, 1953:69).

Presenting the sword and the orb: The sword presented to the monarch symbolizes the power to enforce social order. The sword is a dual symbol of authority and potential destruction to any who would disrupt society. Throughout the remainder of the ceremony, the sword is carried unsheathed in front of the monarch, to remind subjects of "the protection which a good authority can offer them when they themselves adhere to the moral law, and of the wrathful punishment which will follow their deviation" (Shils and Young, 1953:70). The monarch is next given bracelets of sincerity and wisdom and robed. These actions symbolize the transformation of a private individual into a public head of state. Once transformed, the monarch is invested with a sacred orb, symbolic of "the wider sphere of her power and of the responsibilities for its moral use" (Shils and Young, 1953:70).

The Benediction: The duties of subjects are featured in the Archbishop's Benediction which asks God to give the monarch " 'wise counsellors and upright magistrates; leaders of integrity in learning and labor; a devout, learned, and useful clergy; honest, peaceable, and dutiful citizens' " (Shils and Young, 1953:70). The monarch is admonished to obey God, and her subjects are in turn commanded to obey her.

Shils and Young's analysis of the Coronation Service reveals a central theme of church sponsorship of civil religious symbols. The Archbishop of the Church of England, as God's representative, invests the new ruler with authority. The religious investiture of political authority aptly illustrates Coleman's concept of church-sponsored civil religion. According to Shils and Young the significance of church-sponsored civil rituals has not disappeared in the modern era. For example, the last Coronation Service and Procession were widely shared by the British public. The celebration was widely exposed on radio, television, and in magazines and newspaper accounts. Along with the many explanations offered for the popularity of the Coronation (e.g., commercialization and the British love of ceremony), Shils and Young (1953:71) suggest that public interest was motivated primarily by desire for "communion with the sacred." Just as the Coronation Service was a religious event, public involvement also took on aspects of religious ritual. Gift giving, a typical feature of many religious celebrations, was evident in several manifestations. Many subjects sent gifts to the Queen, community organizations gave gifts to children and the elderly, and many people celebrated the occasion by giving gifts within their own families. Shils and Young (1953:75) compare the public festivities to an orgy in the sense that orgiastic expression commonly follows a religious experience.

Shils and Young's observations also reveal examples of the civil reigious function performed by the Coronation. The Coronation Service is a socially integrating ceremony. Public participation in the last Coronation went beyond the level of individual entertainment to become a collective affirmation of societal unity. Family unity, symbolized by devotion to the Royal Family, was also fostered by involvement in the Coronation. But, family solidarity was not reinforced at the expense of national unity. "On this occasion one family was knit together with another in one great national family through identification with the monarchy" (Shils and Young, 1953:73). Shils and Young believe that even class divisions were at low ebb during the time of the last Coronation. They observe that a "degree of moral consensus" has developed in the various classes in modern Britain, along with a "decline in the hostility of the British working and middle classes towards the symbols of the society as a whole and towards the authorities vested with those symbols" (Shils and Young, 1953-76). Class accommodation is not attributed to the Coronation, but the accommodation observed during the Coronation is considered symptomatic of the integrative power of British church-sponsored civil religion. Shils and Young's analysis of the Coronation's integrative function minimizes genuine sources of societal conflict which may not have been evident at the particular time of the Coronation Service. Shils and Young's treatment of British church-sponsored civil religion lacks Bellah's (1975) concept of the "broken covenant" — a civil religion which can both unify and divide society.

Shils and Young cite several examples of the British monarchy's capacity to legitimate other social institutions. Military organizations, in particular, have ceremonial ties to the Crown. Other organizations with royal sponsorship include a multiplicity of voluntary associations, such as the Royal Society and numerous educational and medical facilities (e.g., St. Mary's Hospital and University of London). Sponsorship by the monarchy endows each sponsored organization with a sort of charisma, binding each organization to the structure of the societal moral system. Not only are institutions defined and integrated by the monarchy, monarchical charisma can extend to individual subjects, especially during times of ritual celebration. On the day of the Coronation Service, crowds waited patiently in the rain for some glimpse of the Queen. The legitimacy of the British monarch's authority is derived from a transcendent authority. Each ritual of the Coronation Service is designed to symbolize the monarch's obedience to a higher power. When the Queen kneels before the Archbishop, for example, she indicates submission to God's higher authority. The sword presented to the monarch is the symbol of God's prophetic judgement, to be enacted through the Crown, against any violation of society's laws. Shils and Young's examination shows that the Coronation Service has rich imagery concerning the integrative, legitimating, and prophetic functions of the modern British monarchy.

Shils and Young's analysis of the British Coronation clearly illustrates the form by which church-sponsored civil religion can survive the modernization of a society. In the British case, the constitutional monarchy is recognized as the symbolic authority of the society, and this symbolic authority clearly is derived from the historic sponsorship of the monarchy by the established Church of England. Many British subjects who are not Church of England members, or who are not religious, still participate in the *civil* religious function of the monarchy.

In this respect the British case differs from the situation of a nation like the Soviet Union where the monarchy was destroyed by revolution and modernization. In the U.S.S.R. a system of secular nationalism developed to replace church-sponsored civil religion. Shils and Young suggest that Great Britain did not become a society of secular nationalism because public hostility against political authority was displaced from the monarchy to the leaders of competing political parties. As the political power of the British monarchy slowly declined, its symbolic authority was tolerated and even appreciated by unthreatened politicians. Church-sponsored civil religion might continue to persist in the modern or modernizing state only if its structures are used as an aid to the acquisition and maintenance of political power (e.g., the Khomeini government of Iran) or are considered politically neutral, as in the case of the British monarchy. Despite the decline of the political power of the British Crown, Shils and Young conclude that the monarchy retains considerable social and moral significance for the integration of British subjects, the legitimation of institutions, and the prophetic guidance of the society's course in history.

2. State-Sponsored Civil Religion: Restoration Japan

Civil religion sponsored by the state occurs in societies where the political system institutes a self-transcendent cultus. The institution of a state-sponsored form of civil religion is most likely to occur in a society characterized by competing religious traditions and an authoritarian political system. When no religion is powerful enough to perform civil religious functions for the society, the state may assume these functions to itensify its power and establish its authority. Imperial Rome is an example of a society with state-sponsored civil religion. A modern example is the State Shinto of Restoration Japan. State Shinto was based on the belief in the divinity of the historical line of Japanese emperors. State Shinto was instituted as the state religion of Japan in 1868, at the beginning of the Meiji era, and was not formally disestablished until December, 1945. During this period, State Shinto functioned as a form of religious nationalism despite official claims in later years that the Shinto national cult was not technically a "religion."

The religious origins of State Shinto during the Tokugawa period and of the civil religious functions assumed by State Shinto both demonstrated its essential characteristics as a state-sponsored civil religion. Robert Bellah (1957) found that the historical religious roots of State Shinto could be traced to the primitive, tribal religion of early Japan. Bellah (1957:87) notes that "the earliest Japanese word for government is *matsurigoto,* which means religious observances or worship. This would seem to indicate the lack of differentiation of function between the religious and political spheres." During the Tokugawa period (1600-1868), the historic lack of differentiation between religion and politics continued, manifest in the popular slogan *sonno* (revere the emperor) and the development of the concept of *kokutai* (national body) (Bellah, 1957:99). The ideas of *sonno* and *kokutai* were widespread, promulgated by two intellectual movements, the Kokugaku School and the Mito School. The major religious goal of the Kokugaku School was the restoration of the emperor to power. The ideas of the Kokugaku School proliferated during the nineteenth century and influenced the subsequent Restoration in 1868 (Bellah, 1957:102). The Mito School developed the idea of *kokutai* as "a concept of the state in which religious, political and familistic ideals are indissolubly merged" (Bellah, 1957:104). The resulting national religion was to be centered on the figure of the emperor. Bellah concludes that the ideology of *sonno-kokutai* had an impact on the political modernization of Japan and contributed to the establishment of State Shinto.

The civil religion of Restoration Japan was based on the three dogmas of (1) "divine imperial sovereignty," (2) "special guardianship extended to the land and its people by ancestral deities," and (3) "benevolent destiny" (Holtom, 1947:9, 13, 19). According to the dogma of divine imperial sovereignty, the emperor's bloodline may be traced back to the sun-goddess, Amaterasu Omikami, the ancestress of the Japanese state. The emperor is considered to be divine because he is the direct living embodiment of sacred ancestors of the nation's past. The second Shinto dogma, which holds that the spirits of the sacred ancestors extend a special guardianship to Japan, is signified by the concept of Japan as "the Land of the Gods." The dogma of sacred guardianship affirms that the transcendent nature of Japanese history. From the dogma of ancestral guidance through history, the third dogma of benevolent destiny is derived. Japan is believed to be the "saviour" of the rest of the world. Japan's mission in history is to expand the nation and extend the Japanese way to all other people of the world. The Japanese slogan "the whole world under one roof" symbolizes Japan's "special divine commission to expand sovereignty and righteousness over ever widening territorities" (Holtom, 1947:20). State Shinto, in its basic dogmas, clearly fulfills Coleman's (1970:69) definition of civil religion as a religious symbol system that relates the roles of citizen and society in history to the conditions of ultimate meaning.

The civil religious functions of State Shinto were performed by the Japanese government. The first critical function addressed by the government at the beginning of the Meiji period was that of integrating Japan's heterogeneous population. The feudal heritage of Japan had left diverse rival clans scattered over the countryside. Japan was also religiously diverse. Restoration Japan housed Buddhists, Confucianists, Hindus, Moslims, Taoists, Christians, Secular Shintoists, and adherents of a variety of folk religions. The Japanese government needed an overarching symbol of national unity to integrate diverse local and religious groups, and State Shinto provided this type of unifying symbolism. The newly restored imperial government in 1868 first attempted to establish unity by suppressing competing religions. Buddhism, which was associated with the discredited Tokugawa regime, was criticized. Christianity, a symbol of "Western imperialism," was banned until 1873. Later, under pressure from the West, religious pluralism was officially tolerated as long as the overarching State Shinto tradition was accepted as the highest ethical authority. In order to facilitate religious integration, the Japanese government began in 1899 to insist that State Shinto was not a religion. Japanese Christians and Buddhists eventually accepted State Shinto as a non-competitor and adopted policies of coexistence. The National Christian Council of Japan stated that "we accept the definition of the government that the Shinto Shrine is non-religious" (Holtom, 1947:169). Coleman believes that the religious integration attempted through State Shinto was only *partially* successful, thus illustrating one of the structural weaknesses of state-sponsored civil religion, conflict with historical religions. The dogmas of State Shinto came into particular conflict with the tenets of Buddhism and Christianity, especially the Buddhist doctrine of pacifism and the Christian tradition opposing idolatry (Coleman, 1970:72). Despite the structural weakness noted by Coleman, State Shinto proved to be a powerful integrating force for many Japanese. A traditional avenue of integration, the school was used for this purpose. In 1899, Order Number Twelve was issued by the Restoration government, bringing an end to all specifically religious instruction in public and private schools. Instead, instructions in State Shinto were to be substituted. The goal was the replacement of traditional religion with religious nationalism which would unify the society for the accomplishment of its divine mission (Holtom, 1947:76).

A church-sponsored form of civil religion bestows an established, religiously based legitimacy on a political authority. In the case of state-sponsored civil religion, the political order establishes its own legitimacy by proclaiming the state to be a self-transcendent cult. All institutions serving the national cult are automatically legitimated, and opposing institutions (such as competing religions) are discredited. Yet, State Shinto might never have aroused world attention if it had not been used to legitimate Japanese territorial expansion. The dogma of benevolent destiny, accompanied by an effective military, resulted in the extension of Japanese control to an overseas empire. Japanese hegemony was accompanied by the establishment of Shinto shrines in conquered territories.

The legitimation of Japanese hegemony illustrates another structural flaw of State Shinto and other state-sponsored forms of civil religion. Coleman (1970:72) observes that there "was no humble sense of the nation being under God which would provide leverage for prophetic critique of the civil religion from the organized churches." Holtom agrees that State Shinto was limited by prophetic failure. The Japanese state had functioned like a church "and, like other churches, it was founded on the arrogation that in the last analysis the validity of its decisions were superhuman and supernatural" (Holtom, 1947:176).

The State Shinto of Restoration Japan exemplifies Coleman's ideal type of state-sponsored civil religion. In a society with a pluralistic religious tradition the Restoration government was able to proclaim itself as a national cult in order to perform the functions of social integration, political self-legitimation, and legitimation of imperialism. Japanese Shinto was subject to both of the structural weaknesses Coleman finds in state-controlled forms of civil religion. First, State Shinto provided conflict with competing historic religions, most notably Buddhism and Christianity. Secondly, State Shinto fell victim to its own nationally self-transcendent worldview, which led to the Japanese attempt, and failure, at world domination. The case of Restoration Japan illustrates the structural vulnerability of state-sponsored civil religion when extended beyond the society into the international arena.

3. Secular Nationalism: Modern Soviet Union

Coleman views secular nationalism as a functional alternative to civil religion which is likely to appear "when the historic national religion is either too traditionalistic or too closely tied to prerevolutionary regimes to serve as the civil religion of a modernizing politico-economic regime" (Coleman, 1970:72). Secular nationalism provides a legitimating symbol system which competes with the symbol systems of historic religions. Secular nationalism differs from state-sponsored civil religion primarily in its non-religious or anti-religious self-presentation. Secular nationalism performs civil religious functions for citizens and the society while disclaiming religious significance. The Marxist-Lenninist ideology of the U.S.S.R. is a worldview which "on the one hand can be called a religion and, on the other, is totally opposed to religion in all acceptable forms" (Zeldin, 1969:101). Soviet Marxist-Leninism does not conceive of itself as a religion. It is opposed to traditional forms of religion, and yet it can be observed to perform "religious" functions. The debate concerning whether Soviet communism is or is not a religion can be avoided by adoption of Coleman's term, secular nationalism. The religious functions of Soviet communism are, however, of special interest to the identification of types of civil religion.

Zeldin's (1969:104) analysis of Russian ideology identifies three dogmas that have been transferred from the church-sponsored civil religion of the Czars to Marxist-Leninist secular nationalism; (1) the conception of Moscow as "the Third Rome," (2) the concept of "wholeness, symbolized in the term *pravda*,truth and justice." The messianic idea of "holy Moscow" or "Moscow the Third Rome" developed in the fifteenth century when Rome fell to barbarian invasion and Byzantium came under Islamic domination. Moscow was then considered to be the world center of Christianity. Today, Moscow, now the capital of the U.S.S.R., has become the inspirational center of the Third International. The historic belief in the Czar as the divinely inspired teacher of true Christianity has been transferred to the Soviet Communist Party Central Committee, which is the new source of truth. The ideal of the unity of Eastern Slavs, symbolized in the concept of *pravda*, "is now found in every aspect of Russia communism: in the total integration of life under communism, in the fusing of people into one mass" (Zeldin, 1969:107). Zeldin concludes that significant symbols of modern Soviet secular nationalism are congruent with the symbols of the Czarist-sponsored civil religion of the pre-revolutionary period.

The religious functions of Soviet secular nationalism are apparent in numerous Soviet civil ceremonies, which have been researched by Jennifer McDowell (1974). McDowell (1974:265) classifies Soviet civil ceremonies into two broad categories: (1) private ceremonies such as christenings and weddings, which aid the identity formation of individuals; and (2) public ceremonies, celebrating national or local holidays, which aid social integration. The first Soviet civil ceremonies were established shortly after the Bolshevik Revolution, with new ceremonies being added at various subsequent points in time. The public ceremonies celebrating newly created national holidays, such as January 22 (the overthrow of the Czar), functioned to legitimate and solidify the new regime by clearly symbolizing the break with the past. Private ceremonies, such as the "red baptism" and "red funeral," were established soon after the Civil War but fell into disuse by 1930, only to be officially restored again in the 1950s. McDowell (1974:267) suggests that, in the early years of the Communist regime, the Russian peasants disliked the secularism of the private ceremonies, while Communist Party members and members of the Young Communist League resisted their frivolous ceremonialism.

Soviet scholars, P. P. Kampars and N.M. Zakovich (1967:35-38), present a categorization of Soviet civil ceremonies which assists analysis of the ceremonies' functions. Their major categories are: (1) Revolutionary State Holidays, (2) Laboring Holidays, (3) Civil Rituals and Mode-of-Life Holidays and Rituals, and (4) Traditional Festivals Dedicated to the Times of Year and to Nature, to Work, and to Songs. The first category, Revolutionary State Holidays, includes a variety of national holidays such as Lenin's birthday (April 22) and the anniversary of the Great October Socialist Revolution (November 7). Revolutionary State Holidays celebrate the nation's unique history and offer inspiration for the fulfillment of national destiny. A typical celebration of November 7, for example, includes a military parade, athletic demonstrations, and a civilian parade of 200,000 persons. The mass demonstrations of people, shouting slogans such as " 'Long Live the Inviolable Unity of the Peoples of our country!' " illustrate the integrative function of Revolutionary State Holidays (McDowell, 1974:271).

Laboring Holidays honor the major occupational groups with holidays such as Railway Man's Day, Teacher's Day, Cattle-Breeder's Day, etc., and celebrate the anniversaries of particular collective farms and industrial plants (McDowell, 1974:270). Laboring Holidays function to integrate diverse occupational groups into Soviet society and to reinforce economic achievement. Traditional Festivals Dedicated to the Times of the Year, to Nature, to Work, and to Songs include traditional Russian celebrations such as the New Year's celebration. Traditional Festivals, along with National and Laboring Holidays, have received general popular support and have been successful as mechanisms of integration. Civil Rituals and Mode-of-Life Holidays and Rituals include civil christenings, coming-of-age ceremonies, weddings, major wedding anniversaries, and funeral services. These Civil Rituals have experienced the least acceptance among the Soviet public, especially in rural areas. Despite the conflict of allegiances aroused by private Civil Rituals, available data indicate that these ceremonies are beginning to gain in popularity, due to the decline of traditional religiosity fostered by urbanization. One of the few remaining functions of traditional religion in the U.S.S.R., the sanctification of birth, marriage, and death, is gradually coming under the domain of the civil religion of Soviet secular nationalism.

Upon examination, Soviet Marxist-Leninism is found to be a system of secular nationalism — a functional alternative to civil religion. Although defining itself in non-religious terms, Soviet secular nationalism performs the traditional religious functions of social integration and political legitimation. Due to its self-transcendent stance, however, Marxist-Leninism excludes the role of prophetic protest from its civil religion. Coleman observes that the strains inherent in secular nationalism as a replacement for a transcendent civil religion include persecution of religious citizens and the limitation of religious and civil liberties. Both strains are observable in the modern Soviet Union.

D. Conclusion

Proposition III asserts that civil religious development follows the general direction of cultural evolution. The civil religious systems of four societies, in different stages of modernization, have illustrated the possibilities of civil religious evolution. The key variable Coleman isolates as a predictor of civil religious development is differentiation. Implicit in Coleman's theory is a related variable, religious pluralism. Religious pluralism here refers to something slightly different from simply another manifestation of differentation. Some societies have had fairly low levels of differentiation but have housed numerous major religions with thousands of varying sects. Historic India, Japan, and China serve as illustrations. Other differentiated societies, such as modern Italy, are low in religious pluralism, being dominated by a historically established religion. Figure 10 illustrates that variation in levels of differentiation and religious pluralism may be related to the type of civil religious system in a modern or modernizing society. The level of differentiation ranges from the high differentiation of the most developed society to the low of the modernizing society. Religious pluralism is indicated by a society's history of religious toleration as opposed to an established religion. The secular nationalism of the U.S.S.R. is characteristic of a society with a history of an established religion (Russian Orthodoxy) and a low level of differentiation. Although the modern Soviet Union is approaching a high level of differentiation today, when Soviet secular nationalism was first imposed after the

Bolshevik Revolution, the society was just emerging from feudalism. For secular nationalism to develop under these conditions, the established religion must be perceived as too traditionalistic to perform the civil religious functions for a modernizing government (Coleman, 1970:72).

Figure 10
Coleman's Types of Civil Religion (Coleman, 1970)

Differentiation

Religious Pluralism	*Low*	*High*
History of Established Religion	*Secular Nationalism* U.S.S.R.	*Church-Sponsored Civil Religion* Great Britain
History of Religious Pluralism	*State-Sponsored Civil Religion* Restoration Japan	*Differentiated Civil Religion* U.S.A.

In modern Great Britain, the established church and its historic sponsorship of the monarchy lost power gradually, as the society moved into the modern era. The monarchy, a major symbol of British church-sponsored civil religion, was retained as a powerful national symbol because it threatened no vested political interest. The monarchy was not viewed as a symbol of the failure to modernize, and was viewed instead as the inspiration behind the empire. Thus, in a highly modern society, a somewhat traditional church-sponsored form of civil religion has been retained.

Japan has historically tolerated a variety of religious traditions, including Buddhism, Taoism, Shintoism, and Christianity. Because no one religion was officially established, political interest groups felt required to institute a state-sponsored cult to perform civil religious functions. The symbols of State Shinto were derived from ancient cultural myths, the only Japanese religious symbols with the potential to unify diverse religious organizations. The traditional absence in Japan of differentiation between religious and political institutions (Bellah, 1957:87) also permitted the establishment of a powerful state-sponsored civil religion.

The United States is a highy diffrentiated society with a tradition of religious toleration. Religion and politics have been officially differentiated since the writing of the Constitution. Because no religion was established which would perform civil religious functions, church-sponsored civil religion did not develop. The American revolutionary tradition precluded the likelihood of Americans worshipping the head of state. Therefore, an American form of state-sponsored civil religion would not be expected to emerge. Secular nationalism was also an unlikely choice for the United States, given the Amerian tradition of religiousity and opposition to atheism. Instead, if Propositions I through III are valid the

United States was sufficiently differentiated and religiously plural to facilitate the emergence of a type of civil religion differentiated from religious and political systems, but manifested in these and other institutions at a high level of generality. This chapter has attempted to place the development of American civil religion into a cross-cultural, evolutionary context. All societies can be conceived of as having civil religious functions. In undifferentiated, and even many modern societies, these functions are performed by either an established religion or the state (Coleman, 1970:70). Compared to other societies exhibiting varying degrees of differentiation and religious pluralism, American civil religion can be explained as a differentiated civil religion which developed to perform the specialized religious functions of a modern, plural society. Obviously these functions were not being performed exclusively by either religious institutions or the political system.

CHAPTER 7

CONCLUSIONS AND RECOMMENDATIONS FOR FUTURE RESEARCH

This book has attempted to trace the intellectual development of the sociological concept, "American civil religion," and to order the body of research and theory on civil religion into a set of testable propositions. A survey of the literature reveals that the current state of knowledge concerning civil religion (and especially American civil religion) is primarily theoretical. Philosophers, historians, and social scientists have advanced various theoretical models of American civil religion, folk religion, democratic faith, religious nationalism, transcendent universal religion of the nation, and Protestant civic piety (Richey and Jones, 1974). This conceptual diversity presents a stumbling block to contemporary research. Probably the best-known sociological model of American civil religion, the transcendent universal religion discussed by Robert Bellah (1967; 1975), has stimulated the greatest amount of empirical research (e.g., Thomas and Flippen, 1972; Mueller and Sites, 1977; Jolicoeur and Knowles, 1978; Christenson and Wimberley, 1978; Wimberly, 1976, 1979, 1980; Wimberley and Christenson, 1980). Bellah's model of American civil religion has been productive, due in part to its comprehensiveness. Bellah's concept of transcendent universal American civil religion includes the other basic models of civil religion as elements of a more inclusive model. The research produced in response to it and inclusiveness of Bellah's model of American civil religion recommend it as the point of departure for future research. A concise statement of Bellah's concept of American civil religion is adapted from the work of John A. Coleman (1970), which defines American civil religion as the religious symbol system which relates the citizen's role and American society's place in space, time, and history to the conditions of ultimate existence and meaning. This definition has the advantage of including reference to both the individual and societal levels of analysis and has the potential of guiding sociological research more specifically than have previous definitions derived from philosophical, historical, or early sociological traditions. Three propositions have been derived from Coleman's definition of civil religion, and are restated here.

> *Proposition I:* American civil religion is structurally differentiated from both American religious denominations and American political institutions.

> *Proposition II:* American civil religion performs specialized religious functions performed neither by denominations nor by political institutions.

> *Proposition III:* The differentiation of American civil religion from denominationalism and politics follows the general direction of cultural evolution.

Sociological research on American civil religion has been primarily concerned with the functions performed by civil religious systems and their relationship to other social systems. Coleman (1970) hypothesized that American civil religion is structurally differentiated from both politics and the denominations (Proposition I). Parson's (1971) definition of differentiation, in conjunction with Bellah's (1964) theory of religious differentiation, represents the general theoretical framework from which Coleman's structural differentiation hypothesis is derived. Empirical studies concerning the location of indicators of American civil religion in other social institutions (e.g., Cole and Hammond, 1974; Mueller and Sites, 1977) have provided data in support of Proposition I. The greatest empirical support for the structural differentiation of American civil religion from both religious and political communities is found in Wimberley's (Wimberley et al., 1976; Christenson and Wimberley, 1978; Wimberley, 1976, 1979, 1980; Wimberley and Christenson, 1980) empirical studies of individual civil religious belief. Wimberley finds American civil religion to be a separate, measurable, individual belief dimension which overlaps only minimally with other religious and political beliefs. The limited amount of empirical evidence gathered to date suggests that the values of American civil religion are congruent with the values of American religious and political institutions, although American civil religion is structurally dfferentiated from these institutions. The relationship of American civil religion to other American institutions is not entirely clear. Historical and theoretical studies must be relied upon for the most part, with the exceptions of Jolicoeur and Knowle's (1978) study of American civil religion in a voluntary association and Thomas and Flippen's (1972) analysis of American civil religion in the American press. There is, therefore, as yet little evidence to support the logical hypothesis that most American institutions are in the process of differentiation from both traditional religion and civil religion. The institutions likely to be *least* differentiated from American civil religion are the traditionally integrative institutions such as the family, the schools, and religio-civic voluntary associations. Instrumental institutions, such as the economy and communications media, might be expected to exhibit the greatest degree of differentiation from American civil religion. However, much more research of American belief systems and their location within various American institutions is necessary before the structural differentiation of American civil religion can be confirmed or disconfirmed.

There are conflicting data concerning the functions of American civil religion. Demerath and Hammond (1967), Cherry (1970), Coleman (1970), and Bellah (1967;1975) find American civil religion to be an institutional source of social integration, while Fenn (1976) doubts this. Bellah and Cherry note American civil religion's dual functions of social integration and division, but do not fully specify the conditions under which American civil religion is either integrative or divisive. Bellah also notes the power of American civil religion to legitimate other American institutions. He believes that the legitimating power of American civil religious values has eroded, but affirms the possibility of renewal. In Bellah's view, the myths and symbols of American civil religion are still sufficiently powerful to aid in the interpretation and legitimation of American social experience. Jolicoeur and Knowles' (1978) empirical study of the civil religious values still cherished by Masonic fraternal orders supports Bellah's position. Fenn (1972), taking the position of religious privatism, theorizes that no religiously based system of cultural legitimation, including civil religion, exists for contemporary America. Stauffer (1973) agrees with Fenn on the growth of the private sphere of religion but argues that some mechanism of cultural legitimation must operate even in the most rational, differentiated society. Stauffer finds Bellah's concept of American civil religion to be a useful model of a modern legitimating system. Research on the prophetic function of American civil religion also yields conflicting conclusions. Bellah's model of transcendent, universal, American civil religion contains a potential for prophetic judgement. Bellah's data on civil religious prophecy are primarily historical, as are the supporting data of historian Mead (1967). While empirical research by Wimberley (1976) depicts a transcendent civil religious dimension of personal belief, Bellah (1976a) discounts Wimberley's findings as indicative of public theology rather than transcendent religion. Negative findings regarding the prophetic function of American civil religion come from folk religionists Marty (1959) and Herberg (1955), and one empirical study of Thomas and Flippen (1972). There is not yet sufficient evidence to confirm or disconfirm Propostion II, which states that American civil religion performs specialzed religious functions performed neither by church nor state. Yet, the functional differentiation hypothesis is promising. Even those in opposition to the hypothesis would agree that, in a society characterized by church-state separation, neither religious nor political organizations exclusively sponsor social integration, cultural legitimization, and prophetic guidance. The field is open for other symbol systems such as a differentiated civil religion to assist with the performance of these functions. It is the task of the sociologists of contemporary American society to determine if American civil religion does in fact play a role in the integration, legitimation, and prophetic direction of the society.

If subsequent research confirms that American civil religion is differentiating from religious, political, and other institutions and performing increasingly specialized functions as the religious dimension of the polity, such confirmation will be congruent with the predictions of the major sociological theories of religious evolution. The theories of religious evolution of Weber (1905), Wach (1944), Bellah (1964), Durkheim (1915), and Parsons (1971) each predict increased differentiation of religious symbol systems due to modernization. Following the assumptions of these evolutionary theories, Coleman (1970) predicts the evolution of different forms of civil religion, based on the level of differentiation and degree of religious pluralism. Adapting Coleman's theory to the specific case of American civil religion, Proposition III states that the differentiation of American civil religion from political and religious institutions follows the general direction of cultural evolution. American civil religion may be an expected manifestation of predictable cultural patterns. Currently, there is little empirical evidence relating directy to Proposition III. The best cross-cultural examination of civil religious development is presented by Cole and Hammond (1974). Their data suggest that religious pluralism and high levels of societal and legal complexity are the specific conditions associated with the development of civil religious systems. The United States is the society in which these conditions are manifest to the highest degree and is therefore the society in which differentiated civil religion would be expected to develop. Additional cross-cultural research, extending the Cole and Hammond study, would be necessary before any conclusions concerning evolutionary patterns of civil religious development could be made. The present analysis has been forced to rely on more easily obtainable historical and symbolic studies of civil religion in other societies. Coleman's ideal types of modern civil religious evolution are illustrated by Holtom's (1947) and Bellah's (1957) studies of state-sponsored civil religion in Japan, Shils and Young's (1953) symbolic analysis of church-sponsored civil religion in Great Britain, and Zeldin's

(1969) and McDowell's (1974) research on secular nationalism in the U.S.S.R. These selected cases are only illustrative of modern civil religious development but provide the foundation for more comprehensive and systematic cross-cultural comparison.

The present study summarizes the civil religion literature from several perspectives.Compiling and ordering the existing body of literature facilitates the task of determining future research directions. Today, conceptual debate still characterizes American civil religion theory, hindering the development of precise measurement instruments. Theoretical problems could be reduced by accepting Coleman's (1970) definition of American civil religion and by adopting the conceptual framework advanced in Propositions I through III as the basis for future research. Empirical problems remain. The sociologist of American civil religion is confronted with the task of locating empirical indicators of a generalized cultural symbol system. Thus far, most civil religion research has been conducted through content analyses (e.g., Bellah, 1967; Thomas and Flippen, 1972; Mueller and Sites, 1977; Jolicoeur and Knowles, 1978) and symbolic studies (e.g., Shils and Young, 1953; Warner, 1961; Zeldin, 1969; McDowell, 1974). Continued research of both types will aid the location and classification of civil religion symbols within American institutions. Subjects such as the local celebrations of national holidays are particularly rich data sources for symbolic analysis. Symbolic case studies, however, are limited to the descriptive level of civil religious research, while content analyses can be designed to yield explanatory data. The early content analyses, such as Bellah's 1967 analysis of presidential inaugural addresses, lack the precise measurement instruments and sampling techniques of later studies (e.g., Thomas and Flippen, 1972; Jolicoeur and Knowles, 1978). Unfortunately, reliance upon widely differing measurement instruments has limited the comparability of the recent studies. In two different studies (Thomas and Flippen, 1972; Jolicoeur and Knowles, 1978), the same item was coded as "secular" by one set of researchers and as "civil religious" by the other! A valid and reliable instrument for the identification of American civil religious content is needed. Once such a coding guide is developed, it could be fruitfully applied to the following content areas: United States Supreme Court decisions, United States presidential inaugural addresses, political election speeches, sermons, official journals of religious organizations and religio-civic voluntary associations, commencement addresses, mass advertising contents, and mass communication media coverage of national holidays and times of national celebration and mourning.

A controversial instrument for measuring individual American civil religious belief has been developed and used in a number of studies by Ronald Wimberley and his colleagues (e.g., Wimberley, et. al., 1976; Wimberley, 1976, 1979). Wimberley's items (see appendix) discriminate among other religious and political attitude items when administered to selected and random samples of Americans. Wimberley (1976:348) reports that his items score high on indicators of reliability, but the validity of the items is a matter of debate between Bellah (1976a) and Wimberley (1979). Whether or not Wimberley's scale measures transcendent civil religion or one of civil religion's manifestations as public theology, continued refinement of the scale and application to additional samples should contribute to the field of knowledge concerning variations of individually held American civil religious belief.

The best empirical test of Propositions I through III will probably not come from traditional modes of civil religion research in American sociology. Individual belief studies such as Wimberley's produce data which can only be applied at the individual level of analysis. Although Wimberley's individual belief studies have been cited in this analysis in support of Proposition I, concerning the structural differentiation of American civil religion, this generalization from the level of individual belief to that of social structure is very tenuous. Symbolic studies and content analysis have been limited to the context of one society and have failed to generate the comparative material necessary to test Proposition III, which concerns the cultural evolution of civil religious systems. If the entire proposition set is to be adequately tested, a modern, empirical version of Weberian socio-historical comparison is called for. Cole and Hammond (1974) have made the greatest contribution to this type of research effort in their cross-cultural institutional comparison of world societies. Additional cross-cultural data on civil religious systems need to be gathered to add to the data on societal complexity and legal and religious systems compiled by Cole and Hammond. In a recent theoretical collaboration, Bellah and Hammond (1980) have contributed a comparison of civil religious forms in America, Japan, Mexico, and Italy. It is probable that, if cross-cultural data on civil religion are made available, they will generally confirm Proposition III. It is also likely that the data will reveal that cultural evolution and concomitant civil religious evolution are more complex than Proposition III predicts. For example, in many societies, civil religion will be in the process of differentiating from religious or political domination and will not fit neatly into any of Coleman's ideal types of modern civil religion. Propositions I through III and Coleman's types of civil religion are based on the possible variation of only one variable known to be operant in the process of evolution, differentiation. Inclusion of other variables associated with evolution, such as adaptive upgrading, inclusion, and value generalization (Parsons, 1971) would add complexity to the research effort, but would also generate more comprehensive information concerning the patterns of civil religious development. It is the conclusion of the present analysis that the study of American civil religion can best be advanced by expanding research beyond the boundaries of a single societal case. Cross-cultural research is critical to the compilation of a comprehensive explanation of civil religious development. Cross-cultural research is also necessary for the prediction of the emergence of new civil religious systems and for the prediction of the continuation or decline of the American system of civil religion.

The purpose of this study has been conceptual clarification and theoretical codification, necessary first steps before actual empirical research on American civil religion can be done. It is the conclusion of this analysis that American civil religion is a viable sociological concept, deserving of and fruitful for continued scientific inquiry. Several directions for continuing research have been elaborated with the hope and expectation that the information presented here will provide answers to some of the specific questions of the contemporary sociology of American civil religion.

POSTSCRIPT

Is there a transcendent universal civil religion of the American nation capable of providing sources for the integration of citizens, the legitimation of cultural values, and the prophetic guidance of America's course through history? The evidence has been examined and systematized, yet the question remains unanswered for me. Which version of American society most accurately reflects contemporary reality—the vision of the civil religionists, or the void of the privatists? Both views contain elements of reality. American society can still be observed to exist as a whole, as civil religionists maintain, yet the society also shows signs of the extensive fragmentation documented by privatists. Bellah's image of the "broken covenant" describes the paradox exactly. There is evidence of a civil religious dimension of American society, but the manifestation of the dimension depends upon specific empirical conditions.

I would like to be able to propose an image as powerful as the broken covenant, and to predict the course of American civil religion in the coming decades. I can only offer a hypothesis based on a dialectical evolutionary perspective. I believe that as American society becomes more privatistic the need for some sort of cultural binding force will build. The "end of ideology" will create a void to be filled by another ideology or theology. The result could be the rise of religious nationalism, new emerging forms of cultural belief, or a renewal of transcendent American civil religion. *If* the symbols of American civil religion are renewed, I in no way expect this phenomenon to be a permanent or ultimate trend. I see privatism and civil religionism operating in a dynamic tension in America society. I believe that the study of the interaction between these two trends will generate the greatest amount of insight concerning the future of American society.

Appendix
CIVIL RELIGION ITEMS USED IN THE ANALYSES OF RONALD WIMBERLEY

Civil Religion (Wimberley, 1976:343)

1. It is a mistake to think that America is God's chosen nation today.
2. I consider holidays like the Fourth of July, religious as well as patriotic.
3. We need more laws on morals.
4. We should respect a President's authority since his authority is from God.
5. National leaders should affirm their belief in God.
6. Good patriots are not necessarily religious people.
7. Social justice cannot only be based on laws; it must also come from religion.
8. To me, the flag of the United States is sacred.
9. God can be known through the experiences of the American people.
10. If the American government does not support religion, the government cannot uphold morality.

Civil Religion (Wimberley, 1979:60)

1. The flag of the United States is a sacred symbol.
2. God can be known through the historical experiences of the American people.
3. We should respect a President's authority since it comes from God.
4. In this country, people have equal, divinely given rights to life, freedom, and the search for happiness.
5. In America, freedom comes from God through our system of government by the people.

All items were scored on a 5-point agreement scale.

BIBLIOGRAPHY

Ahlstrom, Sidney E.
1972 *A Religious History of the American People.* New Haven: Yale.

Bailyn, Bernard
1960 *Education in the Forming of American Society.* Chapel Hill: University of North Carolina Press.

Becker, Howard and Alvin Boskoff (eds.)
1957 *Modern Sociological Theory in Continuity and Change.* New York: Dryden.

Bedell, George C., Leo Sandon, Jr. and Charles T. Welborn
1975 *Religion in America* New York: Macmillan.

Bellah, Robert N.
1957 *Tokugawa Religion.* Glencoe: Free Press.

1964 "Religious evolution." *American Sociological Review* 29:358-374.

1967 "Civil religion in America." *Daedalus* 96:1-21.

1973 *Emile Durkheim: On Morality and Society.* Chicago: University of Chicago Press.

1974a "American civil religion in the 1970s." Pp. 255-272 in Russell B. Richey and Donald G. Jones (eds.), *American Civil Religion.* New York: Harper and Row.

1974b "New religious consciousness." *The New Republic* Nov. 23:33-41.

1975 *The Broken Covenant: American Civil Religion in Time of Trial.* New York: Seabury.

1976a "Response to the panel on civil religion." *Sociological Analysis* 37:153-159.

1976b "Comment on 'Bellah and the new orthodoxy.'" *Sociological Analysis* 37:167-168.

Bellah, Robert and Phillip E. Hammond
1980 *Varieties of Civil Religion.* San Francisco: Harper and Row.

Berger, Peter L.
1961 *The Noise of Solemn Assemblies.* Garden City: Doubleday.

1967 *The Sacred Canopy: Elements of a Sociological Theory of Religion.* Garden City: Doubleday.

Berger, Peter L. and Thomas Luckmann
1966 *The Social Construction of Reality.* Garden City: Doubleday Anchor.

Cherry, Conrad
1970 "American sacred ceremonies." Pp. 306-316 in Phillip E. Hammond and Benton Johnson (eds.), *American Mosaic.* New York: Random House.

1971 *God's New Israel.* Englewood Cliffs: Prentice-Hall.

Christenson, John A. and Ronald C. Wimberley
1978 "Who is civil religous?" *Sociological Analysis* 39:77-83.

Cole, William A. and Phillip E. Hammond
1974 "Religious pluralism, legal development and societal complexity: Rudimentary forms of civil religion." *Journal for the Scientific Study of Religion* 13:177-189.

Coleman, John A.
1970 "Civil religion." *Sociological Analysis* 31:67-77.

Demerath, N. J. III and Phillip E. Hammond
1967 *Religion in Social Context.* New York: Random House.

Dewey, John
1934 *A Common Faith.* New Haven: Yale University Press.

Durkheim, Emile
1893 *The Division of Labor in Society.* Trans. by George Simpson 1933. New York: Macmillan.

1915 *The Elementary Forms of the Religious Life.* Trans. by Joseph Ward Swain, 1926. London: Allen and Unwin.

Eckhardt, Roy
1958 The Surge of Piety in America. New York: Association

Eisenstadt, S.N.
1964 "Social change, differentiation and evolution." *American Sociological Review* 29:375-386.

Fenn, Richard K.
1970 "The process of secularization: A post-Parsonian view." *Journal for the Scientific Study of Religion* 9:117:136.

1972 "Toward a new sociology of religion." *Journal for the Scientific Study of Religion* 11:16-32.

1974 "Religion and the legitimation of social systems." Pp. 143-161 in Allan W. Eister (ed.), *Changing Perspectives in the Scientific Study of Religion.* New York: Wiley.

1976 "Bellah and the new orthodoxy." *Sociological Analysis* 37:160-166.

1978 *Toward a Theory of Secularization.* Storrs, Connecticut: Society for the Scientific Study of Religion.

Gist, Noel P.
1940 "Secret societies: A cultural study of fraternalism in the United States." *University of Missouri Studies* 15:9-176.

Glock, Charles Y. and Rodney Stark
1965 *Religion and Society in Tension.* Chicago: Rand McNally

Greeley, Andrew M.
1972 *The Denominational Society.* Glenview, Ill.: Scott, Foresman.

Hammond, Phillip E.
1974 "Religious pluralism and Durkheim's integration thesis." Pp. 115-142 in Allan W. Eister (ed.), *Changing Perspectives in the Scientific Study of Religion.* New York: Wiley.

1976 "The sociology of American civil religion: A bibliographic essay." *Sociological Analysis* 17:169-182.

Herberg, Will
1955 *Protestant, Catholic, Jew.* Garden City: Doubleday.

1974 "American civil religion: What it is and whence it comes." Pp. 76-87 in Russell E. Richey and Donald G. Jones (eds.), *American Civil Religion.* New York: Harper and Row.

Holtom, D. C.
    1947   *Modern Japan and Shinto Nationalism.* Chicago: University of Chicago Press.

Hudson, Winthrop
    1970   *Nationalism and Religion in America.* New York: Harper and Row.

Jolicoeur, Pamela M. and Louis K. Knowles
    1978   "Fraternal associations and civil religion: Scottish Rite Freemasonry." *Review of Religious Research* 20:3-22.

Kampars, P. P. and N. M. Zakovich
    1967   *Sovetskaia grazhdanskaia obriadnost'.* Moscow: Izd. "Mysl."

Littell, Franklin H.
    1962   *From State Church to Pluralism.* Chicago: Aldine.

Little, David
    1970   *Religion, Order and Law.* New York: Harper and Row.

Long, Charles H.
    1974   "Civil rights — civil religion: Visible people and invisible religion." Pp. 211-221 in Russell E. Richey and Donald G. Jones (eds.), *American Civil Religion.* New York: Harper and Row.

Luckmann, Thomas
    1967   *The Invisible Religion: The Transformation of Symbols in Industrial Society.* New York: Macmillan.

McCloskey, Robert G.
    1972   *The Modern Supreme Court.* Cambridge: Harvard University Press.

McDowell, Jennifer
    1974   "Soviet civil ceremonies." *Journal For the Scientific Study of Religion* 13:265-279.

Mackenzie, Norman I.
    1967   Secret Societies. London: Aldus.

Maclear, James F.
    1971   "The republic and the millennium." Pp. 183-216 in Elwyn A. Smith (ed.), *The Religion of the Republic.* Philadelphia: Fortress

Martin, David
    1978   *A General Theory of Secularization.* Oxford: Basil Blackwell.

Martin, Michael W. and Larry R. Peterson
    1978   "Sources of civil religiosity: An exploratory study." Unpublished manuscript, Departments of Sociology, Washington State University, Washington, and Memphis State University, Tennessee.

Marty, Martin E.
    1959   *The New Shape of American Religion.* New York: Harper and Row.

    1974   "Two kinds of civil religion." Pp. 139-157 in Russell E. Richey and Donald G. Jones (eds.), *American Civil Religon.* New York: Harper and Row.

Mead, Sidney E.
    1963   *The Lively Experiment.* New York: Harper and Row.

    1967   "The nation with the soul of a church." *Church History* 36:262-283.

    1975   *The Nation with the Soul of a Church.* New York: Harper and Row.

Michaelson, Robert
    1970   *Piety in the Public Schools.* New York: Macmillan.

Mueller, Samuel A. and Paul L. Sites
    1977   "Calvinism, Lutheranism, and the American civil religion." *Acts of the 14th International Conference on the Sociology of Religion.*

Neuhaus, Richard J.
    1970   "The war, the churches, and civil religion." *Annals of the American Academy of Political and Social Science* 387:128-140.

Niebuhr, H. Richard
    1937   *The Kingdom of God in America.* New York: Harper and Row.

Novak, Michael
    1974   *Choosing Our King.* New York: Macmillan.

Parsons, Talcott
    1966   *Societies.* Englewood Cliffs: Prentice-Hall.

    1971   *The System of Modern Societies.* Englewood Cliffs: Prentice-Hall.

Richey, Russell E. and Donald G. Jones (eds.)
    1974   *American Civil Religion.* New York: Harper and Row.

Rousseau, Jean-Jacques
    1893   *The Social Contract and Discourses.* Trans. by G. D. H. Cole, 1913. London: Dent and Sons.

Schmidt, Alvin J. and Nicholas Babchuk
    1972   "Formal voluntary groups and change over time: A study of fraternal associations." *Journal of Voluntary Action Research* 1:46-55.

Shils, Edward and Michael Young
    1953   "The meaning of the Coronation." *Sociological Review* 1:63-91.

Shiner, Larry
    1968   "The concept of secularization in empirical research." *Journal for the Scientific Study of Religion* 8:207-213.

Sites, Paul L. and Mueller, Samuel A.
    1978   "Bicentennial sermons and the American civil religion." Unpublished manuscript, Departments of Sociology, Kent State University, Ohio, and The University of Akron, Ohio.

Smylie, John
    1963   "National ethos and the church." *Theology Today* (Oct.):313-321.

Stauffer, Robert E.
    1973   "Civil religion, technocracy, and the private sphere." *Journal for the Scientific Study of Religion* 12:415-425.

Thomas, Michael C. and Charles C. Flippen
    1972   "American civil religion: An empirical study." *Social Forces* 51:218-225.

Tocqueville, Alexis de
    1835   *Democracy in America.* Two Volumes. Trans. by Henry Reeve. 1966. New York: Knopf.

Tuveson, Ernest Lee
    1968   *Redeemer Nation: The Ideal of America's Millennial Role.* Chicago: University of Chicago Press.

United States Supreme Court
    1892   *Church of the Holy Trinity v. United States* 143 U.S. 226.

    1925   *Pierce v. Society of Sisters* 268 U.S. 510.

    1930   *Cochran v. Louisiana* 281 U.S. 370.

    1931   *United States v. Macintosh* 283 U.S. 605.

1940   *Minersville v. Gobitis* 310 U.S. 586.

1943   *West Virginia v. Barnette* 319 U.S. 624.

1947   *Everson v. Board of Education* 330 U.S. 1.

1948   *McCollum v. Board of Education* 333 U.S. 203.

1952   *Zorach v. Clauson* 343 U.S. 306.

1954   *Brown v. Board of Education* 347 U.S. 483.

1962   *Engel v. Vitale* 370 U.S. 421.

1963   *School District v. Schempp* 374 U.S. 203.
       Murray v. Curlett 374 U.S. 203.

1965   *United States v. Seeger* 380 U.S. 163.

1968   *Board of Education v. Allen* 392 U.S. 236.

1970   *Welsh v. United States* 398 U.S. 333.

1972   *Furman v. Georgia* 408 U.S. 238.

1976   *Goldstein v. Collin* 99 U.S. 277.

1976   *Gregg v. Georgia* 96 S. Ct. 2909.

Wach, Joachim
1944   *Sociology of Religion.* Chicago: University of Chicago Press.

Warner, William Lloyd
1961   *The Family of God: A Symbolic Study of Christian Life in America.* New Haven: Yale University Press.

1974   "An American sacred ceremony." Pp. 89-111 in Russell E. Richey and Donald G. Jones (eds.), *American Civil Religion.* New York: Harper and Row.

Weber, Max
1905   *The Protestant Ethic and the Spirit of Capitalism.* Trans. by Talcott Parsons, 1930. New York: Scribner's.

1922   *The Sociology of Religion.* Trans. by Ephraim Fischoff, 1963. Boston: Beacon.

Wilson, Bryan
1968   "Religion and churches in contemporary America." Pp. 73-110 in William G. McLoughlin and Robert N. Bellah (eds.), *Religion in America.* Boston: Houghton Mifflin.

1976   *Contemporary Transformations of religion.* Oxford: Clarendon.

Wilson, John F.
1974   "A historian's approach to civil religion." Pp. 115-137 in Russell E. Richey and Donald G. Jones (eds.), *American Civil Religion.* New York: Harper and Row.

Wimberley, Ronald C.
1976   "Testing the civil religion hypothesis." *Sociological Analysis* 37:341-352.

1979   "Continuity and the measurement of civil religion." *Sociological Analysis* 40:59-62.

1980   "Civil religion and the choice for President: Nixon in '72." *Social Forces* 59:44-61.

Wimberley, Ronald C. and James A. Christenson
1980   "Civil religion and church and state." *Sociological Quarterly* 21:35-40.

Wimberley, R.C., D. A. Clelland, T. C. Hood, and C. M. Lipsy
1976   "The civil religion dimension: Is it there?" *Social Forces* 54:890-900.

Yinger, Milton
1963   *Sociology Looks at Religion.* New York: Macmillan.

Zeldin, Mary-Barbara
1969   "The religious nature of Russian Marxism." *Journal for the Scientific Study of Religion.* 8:100-111.

AUTHOR INDEX

SUBJECT INDEX